THE ALTITUDE WITHIN

TALES FROM THE HIMALAYAN TRAILS

RITESSH PANAT

ISBN
Paperback 979-8-89929-311-5
Hardcase 979-8-89929-890-5

CONTENTS

INTRODUCTION

Everest Base Camp@5364m

*Have you ever experienced something in your life
that has changed how you viewed life altogether?*

*Have you met someone in your life that made
you look at life differently?*

*Have you challenged yourself despite the odds, to achieve
something that made you feel wonderful about yourself?*

My answer to all the above is a resounding YES. I ventured upon a journey of a lifetime, hardly knowing at the time, how profoundly life altering it would be.

Sitting at my desk now it almost feels surreal to be filling these pages with the story of my remarkable adventure so that you can have a glimpse into my world and be a part of my experience. Incidentally to begin with, the story starts at the end of my adventure. But suffice it to say though, that we will eventually traverse through the entire length of my journey without leaving out any parts.....

After a short flight from Kathmandu, we reached Delhi airport at around 11 am. Due to the delay in our connecting flight I now had six hours to myself to reflect upon my recent trip to Nepal and most importantly the Everest Base Camp trek....not that I was complaining.

Although the last three weeks were very hectic, they were filled with adventure and excitement and can probably be called one of the best phases of my life. I recall it, as if it was just yesterday that we were in Nepal, looking forward to our trek to the Everest Base camp. Sitting at the airport now as we waited for our flight to arrive, all those days and moments came flooding in a delightful manner into my mind. Physically I was in Delhi but mentally I was still in the Himalayas, walking next to those admirable giants, listening to the beautiful sound of water flowing from the river nearby, surrounded by magnificently large trees and soaking in the calmness and tranquillity of nature.

All the prep that I had been doing for the past one year with its accompanying ups and downs - be it physical, emotional, or mental – felt insignificant on the day we reached the Base camp. It was like my dream had come to life. The feeling one gets when one checks off one of the items on their carefully made bucket list, is very hard to express. And what an achievement it was, from a tiny thought which took seed several years ago up to the moment we actually reached the Everest base camp, was a hell of a journey. The experiences that I had, the people that I met during the trek, the invaluable lessons I learned during the entire process and the unexpected events towards the end of the trek changed the way I look at life now. I will tell you everything about it, in the course of this book.

Revisiting all these memories while I was waiting at the departure terminal took me back in time to 2017, when I had first thought about it. But they say, everything is destined or maybe it's written in our stars even before we were born. There is no way to really determine that, is there? So, maybe my soul always wanted to do this, but my physical body finally caught up to it in 2017 and eventually it happened in 2024. And now here I am, filled with satisfaction, happiness and gratitude towards God for making this possible.

Personally, this achievement was very important and special for me. Not too long ago, I was struggling to climb the stairs at a stretch. I was hesitant to run to catch a train when I was late. I would much rather choose to take the lift than walk up the stairs. I felt exhausted if I ever ventured to use a treadmill for more than two to three minutes. I was heavy, weighing around 105 kgs and due to this I felt very lethargic. Later I was diagnosed with a Thyroid issue. It was so bad that the doctors had to entirely remove my glands. But even after that, it took a while for me to get back to being an energetic person. Though I was never an athlete, in the last couple of years, I became a very dull version of myself. When I think of that version of myself to the current version of me that reached the Base Camp, it feels like an incredible and very unreal journey.

On the trek, I met so many individuals, locals and fellow trekkers that added a colourful dimension to the whole experience. The interactions I had with them; the life stories they shared with me were so inspiring that I could not help but to put them on paper and that formed the motivation to write this book that you hold in your hands. If it wasn't for them, it would have probably just been an ordinary story of me conquering my personal challenges and completing a challenging trek, which I probably would have chosen to keep to myself.

A sudden memory beckons my attention at this moment. A boy from a small village, Pavin, whom I met on the way back. I had the most heartwarming conversation with him that is still etched in my memory. You will meet him shortly for sure. That boy changed my outlook on life. I had made a promise to myself that whatever profit I would earn from this book, I would donate 50% to Pavin. I do not mean to mention it here for you to laud my efforts but to just keep myself accountable.

Without much ado, let us dive into my story that is interwoven with those of so many others.

Let us start with Kathmandu.

CHAPTER I

KATHMANDU DIARIES

Kathmandu

Heaven is a myth, Nepal is real.

I cannot talk enough about the Everest Base camp trek, as by now you must have surely figured out. It was a wonderful and fulfilling experience, an experience of a lifetime.

While I talk about my trip though, how can I not write about the very city I went to for the first time and immediately fell in love with?

Kathmandu, the gateway to the Everest Base Camp and the Himalayas and the Capital of Nepal. Kathmandu is one of the oldest inhabited places in the world, as per Wikipedia.

The city is home to several world heritage sites, including Pashupatinath temple. I had the privilege to visit a few of these places during my stay.

Honestly, I had no idea, that there were so many things to do in Nepal, so many places to visit and activities to do other than the obvious two – scaling the Everest Base Camp and climbing Mt. Everest. Some people visit Nepal on a spiritual journey visiting different religious places in and around Kathmandu. There are so many interesting places to visit here.

Pokhara, known as the tourist capital of Nepal, is one such place. We met a few Germans going to Pokhara as medical volunteers to work in a hospital. Other places that come to mind are the Chandragiri Hills, Annapurna base Camp, Janakpur (Sita's maternal home – who was Lord Rama's wife from the Ramayan), Lumbini (the birthplace of Buddha) and many other tourist destinations. For the people from the subcontinent, it is an easy and economical place to travel and explore.

I was here with two of my friends for the Everest Base Camp – Kappiil and Gavin. One of my friends and I landed at Tribhuvan International Airport, Kathmandu at around 11 am on the 13th of Sept. It took a while for us to understand the visa application process, but the staff who were friendly and efficient were quick to reassure us. As a result, it did not take very long for us to clear immigration. But the real challenge followed soon after.

We were meant to collect our bags and were directed to follow other passengers on the ground floor. The moment we started climbing down the stairs, we saw hundreds of people scrambling to get through the security first, before they could collect their baggage. The security guys did their best to maintain decorum and arrange everyone in a queue, but it was all in vain. It seemed like everyone was competing in some kind of race to clear security checks and get to the other side.

At first, in order to not join the rat race (literally), we waited patiently in the queue, urging others to follow but soon we realised that we may never make it outside if we continued to do so. We reluctantly decided to become a part of the crowd. We pushed to get ahead of the queue and finally managed to clear security checks. It took us a good one and a half hours which involved some wrestling and jostling to get through the process and then pick up our baggage.

Our driver was waiting outside with a placard and so were hundreds of others. Interestingly, there were almost as many people outside as there were on the inside, who had come to receive their friends, families, and/or customers on this sunny weekday afternoon. I could see the eagerness and happiness lining their faces, when they spotted their loved ones. Despite India being the most populous country, I have never witnessed so many people all at once outside Mumbai Airport who had come to receive someone. I am pretty sure that the people in India also love their friends and relatives and care about them in the same way that the Nepalis do. But maybe we as a people, have become more practical in our approach and are slowly losing the significance of these finer nuances in life.

We reached our hotel in about half an hour's time. On the way, the driver adopted the role of a tour guide and started showing us around. We saw (from outside) the Palace where the infamous Royal massacre took place back in 2001- what a tragedy. He also pointed towards, Pashupatinath temple, then the American Embassy building with heightened security, the Casino and so on.

He also briefed us about the places surrounding our hotel. Our hotel was in Thamel, which is where all the tourists usually stay. He told us a fascinating piece of trivia –The people worked for half a day on Friday (interestingly they refer to it as Good Friday) and every Saturday was a holiday in Nepal. Then it was party time.

The traffic was not as dense as I expected. I saw a lot of old Suzuki cars being used as private taxis, mostly Maruti Suzuki 800 or Alto's. I figured that it was possibly cheaper to buy them here, and since they were so compact, they were much easier to navigate and park.

We were welcomed with a nice and cold orange juice which was a welcome respite from the sweltering heat outside. At this point it was just Kappiil and I, as Gavin was supposed to join us a bit later. We settled into our rooms and took a shower and then had our first Nepali Lunch. I can easily say that nothing can beat the Nepali Thali. Freshly cooked Dal, 2 vegetarian curries, rice, curd, papad, and some pickle. Very delicious food and they served a generous quantity.

After our lunch, we decided to take a stroll around. The area was filled with souvenir shops, cafes, restaurants, bars, money exchange counters, small eateries, rooftop bars, massage and tattoo parlours and even shot bars. Evidence of it being a true-blue tourist destination all around us with everything a tourist could ever need or want to buy.

It did not take long for the realisation to set in that we were finally on our holiday (well, just to clarify that this feeling lingered just as long as we were in Kathmandu, not while trekking). Our driver had told us about a club in Thamel which was apparently among the top fifty clubs in the world called Lord of The Drinks (LOD). Eventually, we ended up

One of the temples in Thamel

going there, the same night, how could we resist after his grand claim? Oh boy, what a place, what an ambience, the lights and music were just amazing but more on that later.

Gavin had arrived at around 4 pm and had his shower. He was excited to go out to explore the city and to feel the vibe of being on holiday. We had told him about the club, so it was immediately on our list of places to visit for the day.

If I were to be honest, I never expected anything like this in Kathmandu. We went there at around 9 pm, there were around twenty-five to thirty people there, but no one was dancing. We were already tired due to the long flight, so we decided to call it a night at around 11.30 pm. And that is when the place started to burst into life. It started to get crowded with a few of them dancing to the music, the DJ was at his best, and we noticed that people were queuing up outside to get in.

The streets were flooded with young people, and everyone was heading to LOD. It was like a mandatory ritual on Fridays. Those who could not get in due to capacity, would then go to the Fire Club, the other famous place in the area. And the party apparently goes on until 5 am the next day is what we learned.

We ended our night with a visit to Baskin Robbins, had ice cream and then were off to bed. In Thamel, they have something called tourism police, patrolling 24X7 ensuring the safety of the tourists, managing traffic, and making sure no mishaps happen. I really liked the concept of them being tourist centric. I was told by a retailer, that if there were any brawl or escalation with the tourists, the police would show up in five minutes. I was very impressed.

CHAPTER 2
EXCURSION

Swayambhunath Temple

The following morning, we had a freshly cooked breakfast to fortify us for the day ahead. The service and hospitality were both amazing and so was the food. We all had a good night's sleep due to the fatigue of long flights and even longer layovers. We were now looking forward to visit different places in Kathmandu. Our first stop was at a lovely temple.

Swayambhunath Temple:

After breakfast Nir and Santosh from Ghumnajaau, who were our tour guides came to see us, to discuss the day's itinerary and arrangements. Until that point, we had only ever spoken to them over the phone, so this was the first time we were meeting them in person. We were both very pleased to see each other. In the process of shortlisting a travel company, I must have spoken or interacted with so many people from Nepal. I found that all of them were courteous, humble, honest, and caring. They would advise us based on our need and were very accommodative towards any last-minute changes. Nir proceeded to detail out the trek for us, clarifying expectations during the next two days, as well as during the trek.

Today was specifically reserved for local sightseeing. It was a beautiful sunny day, and our driver was available at our disposal by 1 pm. We first went to Swayambhunath temple, also known as Monkey Temple, mainly because there are more monkeys than you can count on the premises.

The complex consists of a Stupa, a variety of shrines and temples, some dating back to the Licchavi period. The stupa has Buddha's eyes and eyebrows painted on. Between them, the number one (in Nepal script) is painted in the form of a nose. There were also several shops, restaurants, and hostels. The site had two access points: a long staircase leading directly to the main platform of the temple, which is at the top of the hill to the east. There was also an alternate access by road around the hill from the south, leading to the south-west entrance. Since we were there for a trek and needed to maintain fitness levels, we opted to take the stairway, with roughly around four hundred steps. When we reached the top we spent some time there, had some coconut water on the way back and then headed to Kathmandu Durbar square and Hanuman Dhoka.

Monkeys at Swayambhunath

Durbar Square:

The entire complex has a lot of temples including the most famous Kaal Bhairav and Kumari Mata temple and the famous Hanuman Dhoka Museum. The entry fee is 750 NPR (Nepali Rupee) for foreigners and 150 NPR for residents of SAARC Countries. The museum has some rare pics and paintings of previous rulers. It also has personal belongings, such as clothes, statues, centuries-old artifacts, jewellery, ceremonial attire, and other items. After visiting the museum, we had our lunch at one of the food courts and then headed to Kumari Mata Temple.

The Kumari (literally "virgin") is believed to be the reincarnation of the Hindu warrior goddess Taleju, a manifestation of Durga. Buddhists, on the other hand, believe her to be the tantric goddess Vajradevi.

Nepal has several Kumaris, but Kumari Devi, or the Royal Kumari, is the most famous one of them all. Selected in early childhood from the Newar Buddhist Sakhya caste of goldsmiths and silversmiths – potential candidates are placed in a darkened room with freshly severed buffalo heads and dancing men wearing demon masks. It is believed that if the candidate is not frightened by all of this, as most young girls surely would be, she is the next reincarnation of Taleju. Once chosen, she moves into the Kumari Ghar, where her feet will never touch the ground, and she will only leave during specific festivals and religious duties. Each day, however, she makes occasional appearances from her balcony where crowds below wait to see her. As soon as she begins menstruating, or loses blood from an injury, she reverts to mortal status and re-enters society, as the selection process begins again.

We were fortunate enough to see her, during her short appearance which literally lasted for less than five minutes. No one was allowed to take her picture. The temple boasted of very intricate architecture with beautiful wood carvings and was very well maintained.

Pashupatinath Temple:

We then proceeded towards the Pashupatinath temple, which is classified as a World Heritage site and is located near the Bagmati River. This entire temple precinct has a collection of temples, ashrams, images, and inscriptions raised over the centuries along the banks of the river.

The temple is considered to be the other half of Kedarnath Temple, both complementing each other. Kedarnath essentially means the 'Lord of the field'. The main legend associated with the Kedarnath temple is that it was built by the Pandavas – the heroes of Mahabharata. After their victory in the Kurukshetra war, they sought forgiveness from Lord Shiva for all the sins they had committed during the war.

Pashupatinath Temple's existence has been recorded as early as 400 CE. The Temple is a Hindu temple dedicated to Pashupati, a form of Shiva. The temple is considered one of the holiest pilgrimage sites for Hindus. The temple is worshipped as the head of Shiva. His body is at the Kashi Vishwanath in India. As per Shiva Purana, the linga of Pashupatinath that lies in Nepal, has the capacity to fulfil all desires. The temple courtyard has four entrances in the four cardinal directions. The western entrance is the main entrance to the temple courtyard and the remaining three entrances are open only during festivals.

Only practising Hindus of South Asian diaspora and Buddhists of Nepali and Tibetan diaspora are allowed into the temple courtyard. Practising Hindus of Western descent are not allowed into the temple complex and must walk ahead with the other non-Hindu visitors. An exception is granted to Sikhs and Jains of Indian ancestry, who are allowed to enter the temple complex.

On the day we visited it, the place was crowded, and we found that the temple was about to close. We were lucky enough to invoke the blessings of Lord Shiva. We then went to witness the evening prayers on the banks of the Baghmati River. That experience is so deeply engraved in my mind and will remain that way forever which I will get to in a bit.

Pashupatinath Temple

Although it was raining by then, it was amazing to note that there were around three thousand people present there for the Sandhya Aarti (Evening prayer). The Aarti started at around 6.45 pm and went on until 7.30 pm. The Aarati is performed by a group of priests who stand on a platform in front of the temple. The priests hold a series of lamps in their hands, which they move in a circular motion as they chant mantras. They have musicians performing on harmonium, tabla, and other traditional instruments, with the devotees joining them in singing the Aarti. No one attempted to find shelter from the rain. Neither did the priests stop once to cover themselves. The atmosphere felt electric. The enthusiasm and the devotion that I witnessed there, were unmatched and I still remember it vividly to this day.

While all of this was going on, on one side of the river, simultaneously on the other side (bank), I noticed someone being cremated at the same time. While the deceased person's family was performing the last rites and lit the pyre on that side, on the other side the priests were still continuing with their Aarti totally immersed in their prayers.

Two ultimate truths of life lay in front of me, on one side people were seeking moksha via devotion, chanting, and praying and on the other side the person who had passed away, was going through the process of attaining it. The dichotomy of life in that moment was not lost on me. I had tears well up in my eyes as I witnessed this life altering moment. I will never forget this experience and those visuals. If you ever visit Kathmandu, your visit is incomplete without visiting Pashupatinath temple and witnessing the Sandhya Aarti.

The dichotomy on the banks of the Bagmati River

It was almost 8 pm by then, so we decided to have our dinner and went to a place called Sangam Sweets. The food there was delicious. We liked it so much, that a day before our flight to Melbourne, we revisited the place to have dinner there and sample new dishes, ones that we had not tried the last time we were there. A must visit place when in Kathmandu.

CHAPTER 3

RAMECHHAP

Ramechhap is a small village around four to four and a half hours drive from Kathmandu. It is also called Manthali. It has an airport that serves as an alternate option if the Kathmandu International airport is busy or if a flight gets cancelled due to bad weather. During peak season, all flights to and from Lukla operate from Ramechhap, instead of Kathmandu Airport.

The next morning, we had a flight from Kathmandu to Lukla. We were at the airport by 7am, excited and ready to board the flight. While we were there though, we soon realised, to our disappointment that only one flight had taken off. An hour later, there were still no signs of our flight. The airport was slowly but surely getting crowded, all the trekkers from different parts of the world were eagerly waiting for their turn to embark on their adventure. We began talking to some of them. It was lovely to see so many people heading to the same destination with the same objective – to reach the Everest Base camp. It was almost 11 am by then and our excitement gave way to unbridled anxiety. There was a lack of clear communication about the delay or the schedule from the airline staff which left us feeling clueless. Soon a few rumours started circulating that all the flights were now cancelled for the rest of the day, due to bad weather in Lukla. We were still hopeful and stayed put until 1pm when finally, we were told to leave and head to Ramechhap to catch the flight from there, the following day.

We decided to drive to Ramechhap that very same night. We left at 1 am and reached Ramechhap at around 5.30 am. It was a scary but adventurous drive. There were thirteen passengers in our van plus the driver. The entire road zig zagged and went uphill and downhill. We could see the majestic mountains on one side and breathtaking valleys on the other. It was a fun drive, and we were amongst the first to arrive at the airport.

Back in India when I was in sales, I was pretty used to traveling on such roads, so I was not too perturbed by the treacherous journey, but for Gavin and Kappiil they had their heart in their mouth all the way until we reached Ramechhap. Our driver was mercifully very skilled and I know now that it is impossible to drive slowly on this kind of terrain, one has to maintain a particular speed to navigate these winding roads. While I was enjoying it, the others in the van were not even sure if they would ever make it to Ramechhap.

It was a small airport with a small waiting room and a couple of toilets. The airstrip was around a hundred meters from the main building. Since all the flights from Kathmandu were cancelled, all the tourists started to arrive here in Ramechhap. The weather was nice and sunny here, but that was not the only criteria for a flight to take off. The flight is dependent on Lukla's weather, which was our destination.

After spending a few hours at the Ramechhap airport we were told that the weather in Lukla was not good enough for a flight to land, so it was highly unlikely that we would be flying to Lukla on that day. While we were waiting for the announcement, we made a few friends at the airport.

A couple from Bangladesh, a family from Australia, a trio from Malaysia, a group of ten from Maharashtra, India, and a few others and of course we also got to know the airport staff. Ramechhap like I had mentioned was a very small village. Since we would have to spend the night there, our guide managed to book a home stay for us. After lunch, we left our bags in the room and then went out to explore the village. There was a river nearby, which we stopped by first. We played badminton on the river bridge and met some locals. We had some samosas on the way back to our homestay. The facility was average, but the food was really good, the hospitality even better. We had a musical night just after our dinner as that was the only source of entertainment in that town.

On day three, finally the weather cleared out and we managed to take the flight to Lukla. Since our friends took the flight on the same day, we ran into them later, on the trek and I met them again at Lukla airport, on my return flight to Kathmandu. The view from the flight was simply breathtaking. We could see the Himalayan Mountain ranges covered with snow. There were signs of landslides on some of the mountains and the valleys looked beautiful from the top. Landing at Lukla, one of the most dangerous airports in the world, was both exciting and nerve wracking. It involved a lot of precision. Everyone aboard the plane started clapping and cheering for the safe landing of the flight. We had been waiting in anticipation for the last three days to get here. We heaved a collective sigh of relief, now that we had finally arrived in Lukla. We had our breakfast, repacked our bags and embarked on our fourteen-day trek where the first stop was Phakding. That is where we met our porter, Dig Basnet. A young, skinny, tall but fit guy, who would be carrying our duffel bags weighing around twenty-six to twenty-eight kgs for the next fourteen days. What a feat.

Our porter-Dig Bahadur carrying almost
26-28 kgs throughout the trek.

What I learned from the last three days of unanticipated changes peppered in with a few disappointments, was that if we were in the presence of good company and with like-minded people around, we could easily make some great memories, even in a small little place like Ramechhap. My initial return was planned from Lukla to Ramechhap, but due to torrential rains, floods and landslides, I was instead taken directly to Kathmandu from Lukla, which I was grateful for, as it saved me the drive from Ramechhap to Kathmandu.

*"We didn't realize we were making memories
we just knew we were having fun."*

CHAPTER 4

SANTOSH

That is Santosh, enjoying the breathtaking view

During the course of my journey as is expected, I met some locals. While I exchanged merely a few words with some of them, I had some soulful conversations with others, that taught me some important life lessons that entirely changed my perspective. One such person that left an indelible mark on me was our trek guide, Santosh.

So many adjectives spring to mind when I think of this nimble footed human. He was short, skinny, agile, swift, disciplined, honest, hardworking, and committed. He revealed to us that this was his third trip to the base camp. He seemed a bit shy at first, but it was soon overshadowed by his immense wisdom and clarity of thought. His story was not only inspiring but one that would resonate with so many of us.

Though, at first it may seem like a mundane narrative, what makes it unique are the circumstances of his story and the location we were in. Only those who have been to the Everest Base Camp or visited Nepal and its surrounding remote villages or perhaps lived a similar life would be able to relate to this story and appreciate its relevance.

Santosh was born in Palpa, a small village in the Eastern part of Nepal. He has two siblings – a sister and a brother. He is married to a beautiful Nepali girl and has 2 children – a daughter and a son.

His father was in the Indian Army and had fought two wars against Pakistan. It was evident that Santosh had learned discipline due to his father's army background. Despite his father being a proud soldier, he did not wish for his children to join the army. He wished that his children explore the world and learn about life in a different manner.

His son Santosh did exactly that. Soon after completing his graduation, he went to Japan to learn Japanese in a quest to fulfil his dreams. Initially he found it challenging since he had no knowledge of the language or the culture. But in time he adapted, got accustomed to the Japanese way of doing things and learned the language – a testament to his resilience. In the beginning he had often wrestled with the thought of returning to Nepal but his desire to stay, prevailed and eventually he ended up staying in Japan for thirteen years. He had eventually gotten married and had taken his wife with him as well.

He worked in one of the factories there and learned several new skills. Due to his work ethic, he was liked by many and professionally rose through the ranks quickly. He had a good life with a good job, but a realisation slowly hit him. He was not cut out for the structured confines of a 9 to 5 job. He wanted to do something that removed the monotony. He experienced an inner voice that was calling out to him. He decided to pay heed to it, left his life in Japan and moved back to Nepal.

By then his brother was already running a travel company in Kathmandu where he arranged day trips and college tours in and around Kathmandu. Santosh soon joined him. But unfortunately, the timing was not right. Soon after he returned to Kathmandu the dreaded Covid hit and the brothers suffered heavy losses as tourism got affected.

After a couple of years of immense struggle both the brothers eventually found their footing. Now they regularly arrange trips to the Everest Base Camp, Annapurna Base Camp and other local treks and tours.

Soon Santosh realised that this was what he was always meant to do. While his brother managed the administrative side of things in dealing with customers and coordinating hotel and airline bookings, Santosh walks the extra mile (literally) and hiked with the tourists. It is not as easy as it sounds. It not only requires physical stamina but mental agility as well. It needs hard work, discipline, and patience which Santosh has in rich supply. He always thanks his father for this. Being on a trek with tourists can be very challenging. He is away from his family for twelve to fourteen days at a time. It involves tiring days, long walks, high altitude, extreme weather conditions, basic facilities on the trek, limited internet coverage and unknown people to traverse with. But he takes all of this in his stride.

His veteran father had taught him to stay away from fights and had wisely advised him to live peacefully. His father used to share a lot of stories about his time in the army but one would always remain etched in Santosh's mind. Once on the battlefield, his father's friend was injured and his intestines had spilled out, disturbingly hanging from a tree. His father was faced with a choice at that point. He could save himself and leave his friend to die or risk his life in saving his friend. A soldier at heart, his father effortlessly decided on the latter. He managed to push the intestines back into his stomach and carried his friend all the way to the hospital, harbouring hope that his friend would survive.

Unfortunately, though, he did not survive and died the following day much to his father's disappointment. His father did not want this life for his own kids. And that is how Santosh learned how it was best to stay away from unnecessary fights.

I like the way Santosh does this. He says:

If I fight and win, I will get beaten up once I come back home.

If I fight and lose, I will still get beaten up once I am home, so no matter what, it's my loss. So, it's in my best interest not to fight at all.

He wants to live his life pursuing peace and happiness. He wants to give little to no importance to materialistic things. He is a very determined man, like I have said before. He does not eat junk food or sweets, he follows a strict routine, reads a lot of spiritual and religious books among others. He is very committed to his work and to his fellow travellers. He genuinely cares for the people he hikes with and strives to maintain long term relationships.

He dreams of climbing Mount Everest at least once in his life. Despite the demands of his job, he is always found smiling and calm. He finds joy in the little things and encourages others to do the same as well.

This is a perfect story of a village kid who finished his education, went abroad to pursue higher education, lived a fulfilling life in Japan, left all of it to pursue an inner calling, returned to his home country and is now doing what he is passionate about.

His explanation about this is very simple:

---

*Happiness is not what's outside,
it's within, all you have to do is explore it.*

CHAPTER 5

PAVIN

Now that you have read about Santosh, who decided to leave his overseas job and well-established life to pursue happiness and his inner calling, I want to now tell you about a sweet, wonderful boy called Pavin. The objective of these individual stories is to present some personal journeys and the lessons that we can learn (I have learned) from their lives and experiences that we can benefit from ourselves, in one way or another.

I met so many individuals and groups of people from so many countries during the trek. Everyone had their own unique reasons to travel to the Everest Base Camp, as I had mine. But it was not just about those travellers, their experiences and their lives, it was also about all those local Nepali people I met and interacted with, while I was following my dream to reach the Everest Base camp. I wanted to highlight the way they survived in the harsh conditions of the mountains. Often, trekkers or storytellers focus on their own challenges and motivation for the trek, overlooking and failing to adequately acknowledge the local people, their contributions, challenges, and hardship.

On one such beautiful day while walking back from Pheriche to Phortse, I met a young kid who was on his way to school. His name was Pavin. He was eight years old and was in grade three. His school started at 10 am every day. He left home every day at around 8.45 am. Since he lived in the mountains the path to his school was obviously not a straight one. He had to walk down the hill first and then climb up to go to the school on the other side. And he did this zealously every day, most of the time alone or sometimes with his classmates. He had twelve other kids in his class.

I spoke to him in Hindi. I could tell that he understood the basic questions, like, what his name was, where he was going and how old he was. By that time though, I was curious to know more about him, so I asked my tour guide to converse with him in Nepali. We offered him some snickers and some lollies.

The small village in the background is Pavin's home, Shomare

And I got my second story from there. Very inspiring, full of positivity and hope. This is what I learned about Pavin.

Eight-year-old Pavin lived with his mum in Shomare village, a very small town in between Pheriche and Pangboche. His father had left them (his mother, his thirteen-year-old sister and Pavin by themselves) and had gone to India. His mother ran a tea house in Shomare to support the kids and herself. Pavin's elder sister lived and studied in a small village named Sherkam, to take care of his grandmother who was blind. The nearest big town/village, Namche Bazar, was at least at a walking distance of about seven hours. There was no public transport, no roads nor any trains to get there. If anyone wanted to go to Namche or Lukla or to Kathmandu, walking was the only option, unless one could afford a helicopter ride, which most of the locals obviously could not.

For most of us, this might sound like a familiar scenario, nothing that we have not heard before, but what makes it even more difficult and heartbreaking is the conditions he lived in. Imagine living at around four thousand metres above sea level, in severe weather conditions. His mother's tea business was basically seasonal. There was no guarantee that any trekkers would stop by her tea stall as there are several enroute. Those who lived in these kinds of conditions or those who had been there and witnessed all of this, knew what it took to survive.

Despite all these odds, Pavin was very determined to study hard to make his mum happy. He said, if he did not come first in class, his mother would beat him. This kid was so charming and very well raised by his mum. Once school was over, he would then go and help his mum in the tea house. He was friendly, confident, mature, and very social for his age. I never noticed any hesitance during the entire conversation, nor was he nervous – evidence of him being around tourists a lot. When he spoke about his family situation, I could somehow feel his pain, but Pavin was very practical and clear about the current state of his life, and in a way, it looked like he had accepted his lot. The above picture is the proof of all those qualities. Instead of cribbing and crying, the best way to live life in such situations is to embrace it and try to make it better is what I learned from that little boy.

Though he was too young to understand the complexities of life as they were, I was pretty sure, it was not easy for him to stay positive and happy all the time and neither was it for his mum and sister. But such was life in Nepal for his family and so many others who lived there. It took a lot of effort to stay happy, stay positive and confident especially when they are in pain and had such huge challenges in their lives. And I sincerely admire them for this quality.

When I met Pavin, I was directed to the below lines, from an unknown author.

Do not let adverse situations leave impressions in your mind and take your happiness away.

Shrug them off and stand tall.

After bidding goodbye and receiving a sweet kiss from him, I saw him, as he trotted off to school and we soon moved on to our next destination, Phortse, where another story was brewing which, at the time we had no idea of. But Pavin and the conversation I had with him, is still as fresh on my mind to this day as if it had happened just yesterday. I don't think I will ever forget that precious boy.

CHAPTER 6

LHAKPA

Lhakpa (on the right) in his lodge

My initial plan was to just write about my preparation and personal experience at the Everest Base Camp Trek that I completed in Sept 2024. It was meant to be just one story. But when I landed in Kathmandu and started my trek, I met so many individuals and groups from all over the world that I realised, there was a story in each one of them. Some interactions turned into life lessons; some characters were so inspiring that I still think about them every day. So, I decided to add my story at the very end but instead capture all these beautiful connections first.

The previous two stories were dedicated to Santosh, my tour guide and Pavin a cute, happy, confident young kid who inspired me to stay positive, confident, happy and content, no matter how difficult and challenging life was.

This story is about grit, passion, commitment and social responsibility. On the way back from the Base Camp to Namche Bazar, my guide took me through an off-route town. So, from Pheriche we went to Phortse via Pangboche instead of the usual Tengboche route. I must admit, it was very tiring but equally rewarding. Not only was the view spectacular, but we also ran into Pavin from my previous story and later into Lhakpa in Phortse, the hero of this story.

Lhakpa is a Sherpa, he is twenty-nine years old and climbed Mount Everest twice so far. He was just twenty-one when he had climbed the Highest Mountain on earth for the first time. Lhakpa means Wednesday, coincidently the day we met him, was a Wednesday. Sherpas names include the day of the week they were born. Nima means Sunday, Pasang means Friday and so on.

After a long and tiring walk that lasted six hours, we reached this small but beautiful village, Phortse and went straight to one of the Tea Houses for lunch. We were both exhausted and hungry in equal proportions. We barely had any stamina to talk to anyone about anything, as we still had to walk for another three and half hours to reach our destination where we would finally sleep for the night.

This young gentleman took our order and left. He appeared forty-five mins later with freshly cooked potato curry mixed with carrot and some green veggies, dal and rice. The meal was hot, fresh, and delicious and served with love. We spent those forty-five mins that we were eagerly waiting for our food, exploring the room, the outdoors and resting for a bit as well, as our bodies were exhausted.

With the sumptuous food in our bellies, we began to talk to the man who had initially taken our order. Only then did we realise the person we were talking to had climbed Mount Everest twice as a sherpa. His father had been a leader and had climbed Everest fifteen times, leading several expeditions. His father and mother now lived in the USA.

Lhakpa climbed Everest from both the North (Tibet side) and from the South (Nepal side). He also managed the Phortse Guest House and Restaurant during the season and did a bit of farming during off season, mostly harvesting potatoes.

He had a small room which served as a museum and displayed his father's equipment and tools used during the Everest Expedition. A wallpaper with a view of Mount Everest was hung up on one of the walls. His personal equipment on a board also displaying different types of knots hung majestically on another wall. Needless to say, it gave me goose bumps. Until then I had never met anyone who had climbed Mount Everest. Lhakpa did his best to satisfy my curiosity.

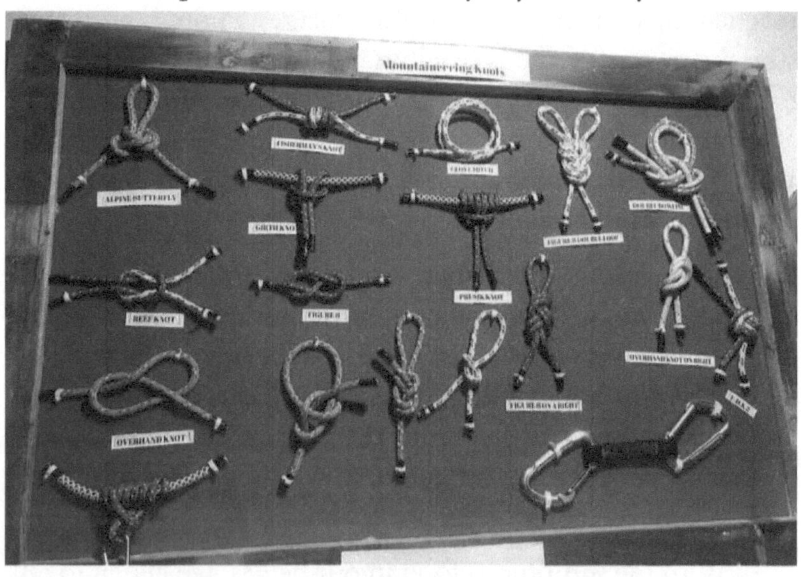

Different types of knots from the museum

He eventually went on to explain how the potato trade worked in this region, especially when there was no motor or train transport available. The only option was to load them on yaks or donkeys or alternately they were carried by men on their backs, in small quantities.

He then took us to the neighbouring building which hosts the Khumbu Climbing Centre. This was inaugurated in June 2019 in collaboration with Alex Lowe Charitable Foundation and Khumbu Climbing Centre. Lhakpa is one of the instructors in the centre, which trains sherpas in technical skills and climbing skills. They provide hands on coaching to sherpas from all over the world. As per Lhakpa, they have trained around five thousand sherpas since the Centre was first inaugurated. It is a not-for-profit foundation and charges very minimal fees for training. Apparently on an average, Phortse produces a greater number of sherpas as compared to any other regions in Nepal. And eighty percent of sherpas from Phortse had summited Mount Everest. When Lhakpa was talking to us, I could see enormous pride color his face. He was so passionate about the mountains and climbing. He genuinely wanted to train sherpas in a way that would not only benefit them but also the wider trekking community and the environment. He could have easily chosen to migrate to the US along with his parents, but he selflessly decided to stay put and help others to fulfill their dreams instead.

Listening to his thoughts and feeling his infectious enthusiasm, we were left stunned and in awe of the man who looked so unassuming at first. Had we not taken that detour, we would have missed this story of self-belief and determination, of someone who wanted to train more people to be good sherpas and proudly take forward the legacy of his father.

Grit is passion and perseverance for long-term goals.

Grit is having the stamina.

Grit is sticking with your future, day-in, day-out.

*Not just for the week, not just for the month,
but for years on end.*

And working really hard to make that future a reality.

Grit is living life like as if it's a marathon, not a sprint.

CHAPTER 7

HEROES ON THE MOUNTAINS

Travelers from all over the world

Travel is like an endless university. You never stop learning – Harvey Lloyd

This statement completely resonates with me. I have observed and learned more during my Everest Base Camp trip than all my previous travels put together, not that I have travelled a lot. This time it was somehow very different. In interacting with the locals and understanding more about their lives, I hardly felt like a tourist, but I felt more like I was one of them – the people of Nepal. I had the opportunity to interact with tourists, trekkers, locals, hotel staff, cab drivers and shop owners. They all were from different parts of the world, some from the UK, US, New Zealand, Australia, India, Israel, Iran, Brazil, Myanmar, Singapore, Germany, Russia,

Bulgaria, Poland and of course some local Nepali people as well. So many nationalities who shared one thing in common – an eternal love for the mountains and a compassion for others.

Some were on this quest as they wanted to prove something to someone in their lives or perhaps even to themselves, some were merely adventurous or enthusiastic. Some of them were determined, passionate and were prepared for the rough and rigid terrain with the knowledge of what they were getting themselves into. And some were just kids, their parents had got them to the mountains to trek for eleven to twelve days.

I met one such family from Arizona, USA. A mother, a father and their two kids - a boy aged thirteen and a girl aged eleven. Observing the kid's enthusiasm, I was tempted to talk to them to understand what was going on in their mind. I learned that the family had come to Nepal from Morocco after staying there for a couple of months. They would be staying in Nepal for three months and then heading to India for another three months. They wanted to know about some tourist and non- tourist attractions in India that they could visit during their stay there. We willingly provided them with the information they were looking for. We even suggested that they keep Mumbai towards the end of their trip, so that it would be easy for them to catch a flight to the US. To my surprise the lady told us that they were not intending to go back to the US just yet.

The family from Arizona

They wanted to go to Sri Lanka or Mauritius then to Greece and then Africa. They were on vacation for fourteen whole months, travelling all over the world, with no jobs holding them down and no school to send the kids to, during that duration. I was so sure that the kids would learn way more in those fourteen months about Geography, History, Physics, Business, Maths and Humanity than they would have ever learned sitting at their desk at school. Their story left me feeling stunned. I asked the girl what she had found to be the most interesting thing in Morocco and she promptly said, 'A monkey pinched me', eliciting a laugh from me. Kids can be so innocent and genuine. But I am sure, she would remember way more things than just that monkey and she would have a lot of stories to tell her friends, relatives back home and to the generations to come.

We met another interesting guy from the UK, Steve. He had come with ten others in a group. He did not look like he was the fittest in the group. In fact, he looked a bit overweight compared to the others with him. But he was walking at a steady pace with sticks in his hands and a guide just to himself. In all the places that they had mapped out, he would be the last person to arrive by the evening, yet the entire group would cheer for him and encourage him. He was neither bothered nor frustrated, that his group had left him alone and that he had to walk by himself. I later learned that he had a hip replacement done a few months ago, but he was still committed and determined that he wanted to attempt the trip and finish the Everest Base Camp, which he finally did accomplish. Whenever we had a second thought about the trek, he encouraged us to keep going. What an inspiration he was.

The girls from Brazil

We also met two young and very enthusiastic girls from Brazil who now live in Ireland. They came by themselves, no guide, no porter, carrying almost ten to twelve kgs on their back. It was Trish's wish to do the Everest Base Camp. She had a screensaver on her phone to remind herself of her dream since the year 2017. She had met with an accident a year before she decided to go on the trek and had injured her knee, that she was still recovering from. But one of her friends agreed to join her and despite the injury and pain, she could not resist the opportunity to travel and she managed to reach the Everest Base camp without any issue. That according to me is the epitome of determination and passion.

I am reminded of yet another interesting story at this point. That of a daughter and her father who was sixty-two years of age who were on the trek with us. They were from Myanmar. They were sitting quietly enjoying their evening tea in one of the lodges, when I began talking to them. Apparently, the father was watching some EBC trek videos three to four weeks ago and asked his daughter if she would be interested to head there. She immediately agreed and that was the reason they both were there. No long-term planning, practice, nothing. Just sheer enthusiasm and self-confidence. Even at sixty-two, he was still energetic and funny, he also sang a song in his language to cheer us up.

I must give you a bit of context before getting into my next story. Khumbu region in Nepal is very harsh. The only mode of transport is a flight to Lukla, either from Kathmandu or Ramechhap and then the only way to get anywhere is to walk. Usually when the people who live in Namche Bazar or Lobuche or even in Gorakshep (the last and highest village before EBC), go to Kathmandu for shopping or during off-season, they are left with no option but to walk to and from Lukla.

During our trip there we met two ladies who were heading back to their home village after seven years with their dad, who was sixty-five. The village they were heading to, was Thukla which is 4600 metres above sea level. It would take them three to four days to reach home, walking almost six to seven hours a day. Yet all three of them looked so joyous that they were visiting their hometown after so many years. No matter how difficult and painful the walk seemed to be, just the thought of getting back to their roots and to their own people felt so reassuring and fulfilling to them that nothing could dampen their spirits. Hats off to them and to all those living in that region.

*"Traveling — it leaves you speechless,
then turns you into a storyteller."*

Ibn Battuta.

CHAPTER 8

THE PRECURSOR

Mount Everest

Seeds:

All of us are familiar with the tallest mountain on earth. Most of us also know who had climbed that mountain first. And yes, you are right, it is Mt. Everest and Edmund Hillary respectively. It would be A life-changing moment if one were to achieve that feat at any time in their lives. But for me, this achievement would probably be something that I leave for another lifetime. In this lifetime the closest I could get to Mount Everest, was by doing the Everest Base Camp trek. Wherein I could see the mammoth mountain majestically towering in front of me to almost 8,850m.

Going to EBC is a bucket list item for so many, just like for me. Especially after one of my friends went, back in 2017, I was inspired to attempt it myself. Life unfortunately took a sharp turn in 2018 and my plan got instantly derailed. The thought slowly faded away into oblivion. I had recently been separated after my divorce and I soon found myself grappling with fresh challenges in another relationship. My circumstances became even more complicated as I began to struggle financially as well. Talk about a grim situation. Mentally I was so consumed by the pitfalls in my life that I had no time to think about anything else but how to survive my ordeal and get out of my situation. Every day felt like a struggle. I was working tirelessly, almost sixty to sixty-five hours a week which translated into approximately 250 hours a month.

On top of that, things were not going so great health wise either. I had a couple of surgeries in the year 2020 and then again in the year 2021. I had carpel tunnel surgery on one of my hands in 2020. I had the same issue on my other hand in 2021 and had another surgery, that also included the replacement of one of my cervical discs. If I were to be completely honest, I had experienced pain and associated symptoms for at least eight to ten months before my first surgery, but it was several months later that I finally decided to do something about it. By then things had already become grave enough to necessitate surgery. A word to the wise – always take care of any niggling pains or symptoms right off the bat to avoid what happened to me. It took almost six months for me to recover after each surgery. As if that was not enough, I suffered from severe back pain in Jan 2023. It was so bad; I could barely walk for a couple of days without any support. And all of this occurred during peak Covid. I owned a fast-food restaurant in 2018 that specialises in Portuguese cuisine, in one of the shopping centres in Melbourne. During Covid, which we all know, lasted for about two years, came with its own set of challenges. My restaurant closed down for a whole year during that time just like several others all around the world, which meant a loss of business and revenue which was terribly unfortunate. I just could not see the light at the end of the tunnel. I barely had any reprieve from all of this to think about even taking a nice short holiday, forget about doing the Everest Base Camp.

But it was constantly nagging me, and I knew that the tiny thought would not leave me. It was waiting in the shadows for an appropriate moment to surface. And predictably it did so in 2023. By then, I was still managing my restaurant on the weekends and was also working at full time job on the rest of the days in the week where I worked as a billing specialist in the Utility Sector. I was living in a shared accommodation with a guy named Kappiil. He was a trekker and a hardcore one at that. He used to go on four-to-five-day treks, hiking, and camping in the New Zealand mountains. Walking with just a backpack, a tent and enough food and water to survive for three to four days. So, in 2023 when I spoke to him about my idea to travel to the Everest Base Camp, he sounded as excited as I was, about the prospect and we soon decided to make arrangements to travel in 2024. We wanted to do this before we hit that big five 0. We began to plan for our trip by Nov 2023. One of Kappiil's friends also agreed to be a part of our expedition, so eventually it ended up being the three of us who went to the mountains with a common goal and a destination.

Planning:

The first thing to do was to find someone who had done this before, so that we could get firsthand information directly from them. I knew someone who had been to the base camp in 2017, but I was not in touch with him. Kappiil could not find anyone either. So instead, we started watching some YouTube videos, of trekkers who had done this before. Some of the videos were very detailed and helped us understand the terrain better, how easy or challenging it would be and what preparations we needed to make before we landed in Kathmandu.

I was never an athlete or a jogger or a trekker. I used to walk every now and then, but it was more like a casual walk without any purpose. Although I was healthy, I had lost my grip and a bit of strength in my hands due to the aforementioned surgeries. So, for me it was a challenge to motivate myself to get ready for the twelve to thirteen days walk or trek and high-altitude weather and to physically prepare myself for this challenging task. Other than mental and physical commitment, the other aspect for me to prepare were my finances, in order to afford the trip. A rough estimate was that I needed at least AU $5,000-$6,000 (Australian Dollars) and some contingency funds for the trip and three weeks of annual leave from work, which I had. Thankfully we did not have to pay the entire sum at one go and had enough time to arrange and save the money.

Blocking dates & Task Distribution:

We agreed to distribute the various tasks amongst us, Kappiil being an experienced hiker, was tasked with planning our practice hikes. So, he was the one to decide when, where and how many times we would go. As a veteran, he would also let us know what equipment and clothing we would need for our adventure as well. Gavin oversaw getting overseas insurance as well as the photography during the trek. I took the initiative to get in touch with various travel groups from Nepal to understand more about the cost, trek, requirements, the dos and don'ts, inclusions and exclusions and the best timing of the year for the trek. I was also tasked to explore and book our travel tickets to and from Kathmandu from our place of residence, which was Melbourne. We were told that the best time of the year to get there was either from March to May or from Sept to Dec. If we went by March, we realised that we would not have enough time to plan the trip, so we locked it for Sept 2024 instead.

The only dynamic component of the entire trip was the cost of the flights, so we decided to book the tickets first and then figure out the rest of the logistics which was to book the tour guide and other items on our list. After looking at various dates and options, we finally booked our tickets for 12th of Sept and a return flight on the 1st of Oct by Malaysian Airlines (spoiler alert – a twist awaits). This was the shortest flight available at the time and the cheapest as well. We paid $1300 per head for the flight. Now that the tickets were booked, we were certain that we would be flying to Kathmandu and now we could focus on other aspects of the trip - to practice, shop for clothes and equipment, conduct further research and get our health insurance. A vital part of the whole trip was to train ourselves and get into a physically fit form for the trek. So, we decided that during the week everyone would practice individually, when they found the time but once in a fortnight, we would go on a trek or hike together. That way, we had the flexibility to do things according to our convenience, but we also ensured that we would get to meet and practise together as a team. It was a system that worked well.

Practice:

We began practice in Jan 2024. The first thing I wanted to do was to get in shape. So, I started working both on my diet and fitness. I went on walks at least three to four days a week. I initially started with walking for about five kms and then slowly expanded my radius to seven km and later began to walk for about ten to twelve kms a day. On an average from Jan to July, I completed about two hundred and twenty-five thousand steps on average in a month, including a couple of hikes in the mountains. The You Yangs range was very close to our house, as well as the Werribee Gorge circuit. Both the tracks mirror at least sixty to seventy percent of the EBC trek, in terms of difficulty and variations. We also accomplished a thousand steps in the Dandenong range a few times, which was a bit challenging to be honest. From Jan 2024 to Sept 2024, which was just a little before our trip, I managed to lose a whopping twelve kgs, and almost twenty kgs since I suffered from my back issue in Jan 2023. At that point I felt so much lighter and energetic.

When I went to India on a short trip in April, I did some shopping there and obtained the rest of the items back in Melbourne. The three of us even got ourselves a printed T-shirt for D-day.

Everything was going smoothly until that point. Our tickets were booked, shopping was in full swing, we were getting into the routine of regular walks and weekly hikes and all of us were very pumped up, eager to board the flight and start the trek. But an unexpected event put a spanner in the

Kappiil and I at the You Yangs Range

wheels and derailed our enthusiasm. I lost my father in July. It was so sudden that I did not see it coming at all. He was diagnosed with stage four cancer and passed away in less than two weeks from the day we got his medical reports, which, was too little a time to process everything. Within twenty-four hours I was in India. It was very shocking, as I had just met him a couple of months ago. He was very happy back then, as he had met most of his relatives for a function at home and he looked totally fine. I mean, he had his challenges, but looking at him then, no one could tell that he was battling cancer internally. I guess, it deteriorated so fast that we had no time to act on it. You never really know that the last time you meet someone could be the last time.

Since I was busy in the rituals as well as my work, I obviously could not practice at all for that entire month. I was not sure as to how this would affect me on the trek, but I was still determined to continue with the prebooked dates. I had taken my father's ashes with me after the funeral and later after the trek, I immersed it in Kathmandu in the Baghmati River, behind the Pashupatinath temple, as I knew, he would have been very proud of me achieving the milestone of the Base camp trek.

Our flight to Kathmandu was exactly in a month's time, after I returned to Melbourne from India. I did my best to practice as much as I could. Again, what's the fun, if everything goes as planned right? Just two weeks before our flight, Malaysian Airlines decided to cancel our flight from Melbourne to Kathmandu without giving us any alternate option.

The way things were going with first my father's death and then the flight getting cancelled at the last moment, I thought the universe was trying to tell me something. Would there be any bigger challenges or danger ahead of me? Am I still supposed to stick to my plan and attempt the trek or should I back off for now, rethink and reschedule it for another time? I even recall suggesting to Kappiil and Gavin to continue their trek without me, which they were not ready for. They refused to go without me citing that it was a team thing. I was in two minds. After listening to them and with everything that had occurred in my life to that point, I was ready for any challenge. I thought to myself what else could go wrong? And secretly hoped the universe would not answer that question. So, we finally decided to look for other airline options. After a lot of back-and-forth negotiations and verbal altercations, they managed to reschedule Gavin's flight, with a thirteen-hour layover in Kuala Lumpur and thankfully he got his rescheduled ticket at the same price.

I was so frustrated and angry in dealing with the airline. But here I was merely two weeks from boarding the flight, and I found myself scrambling to find another option. It was exactly five days before our scheduled flight when we finally managed to rebook ourselves.

Kappiil and I had no option but to cancel the tickets and rebook ourselves on a different airline. And that too after paying AU $1,000 per head, over and above what we paid initially. Despite my previous oath, that I would not travel on Air India, at least for the next three to four years, we had to reluctantly book our tickets with Air India (never say never again–lol), as that was the cheapest and fastest flight to Kathmandu on that day, but with a thirteen-hour layover in Delhi.

Air India was consistent with their substandard aircraft facilities and services. I found only two things on this airline that one could consider mildly appreciative. First that it flies and second its food. After a twelve-hour direct flight to Delhi, we stayed in one of those sleeping pods at the Delhi airport. It was alright, for that price, we paid INR 7000, for a double bed pod. The other option was the Holiday Inn Express inside the Terminal, but the cost was almost INR 14000, without breakfast. Or we could have gone and explored Delhi for seven to eight hours to return just before our flight to Kathmandu, but we realised that it would end up getting very hectic and unnecessary.

We wanted to get some rest as we had no clue how the trek would go. The sleeping pods had single and double bed options. It seemed very basic and experimental at the time. Very small pods, just enough space to keep your bag and possibly a fan. When we lay down, we could see the airport roof. We could hardly sleep, as it was really hot. Apparently, the air conditioners were not working for the last twenty-four hours. But we just wanted to rest for some time. The next morning, we had a south Indian breakfast and filter coffee at one of the food stalls and were soon ready for our next flight to Kathmandu from Delhi, which was an hour and fifteen minutes. After some delay, we reached Kathmandu at around 11.30 am. With the last-minute flight cancellations and all the trouble, we went through to rebook and get our refund, we were just hoping that everything from here went on smoothly. But we were wrong – of course. Destiny had other things planned for us as you will soon see.

Stay tuned for the actual action on the field and the climax........

"Unexpected events can set you back or set you up.
It's all a matter of – perspective."

CHAPTER 9

LIGHTS, CAMERA, ACTION

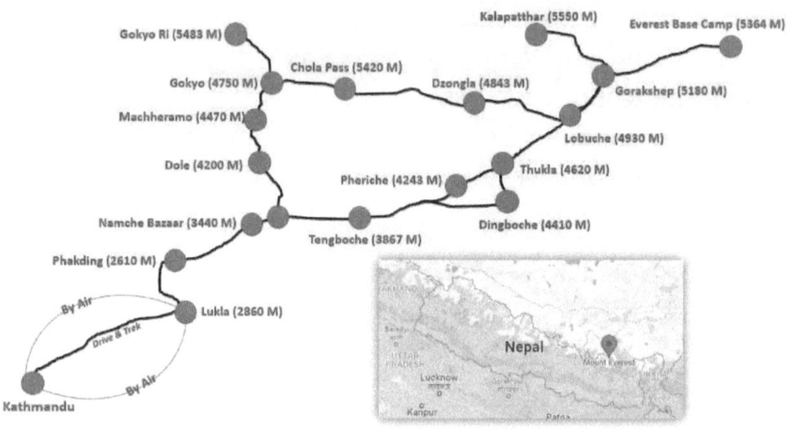

Our Original route to the Base camp then to Gokyo and back.

On the base camp trek, there is a place called Chukla Lare, which is a memorial site, honouring all the climbers and sherpas who have died attempting to climb Mount Everest. I had read the quote that you see here, on the memorial stone of a hiker called Don Cash and it rang so true for me. Don had conquered the Seven Summits — the tallest mountains on each continent. He died on Mt. Everest shortly after reaching the peak in 2019.

Don Cash memorial

At one point just dreaming of the Everest Base Camp was scary and challenging for me. I had never planned to scale it. It all boiled down to two reasons – One was that I hated the winter and the cold and the other was that I had never been an athlete nor a trekker, so I had no idea if I had what it took to attempt the trek.

But here I was several years later, in Kathmandu for the same, with my friends Kappiil and Gavin. During my research, we had zeroed in on our tour guide. We opted for a trekking company called Ghumnajaau Tours. It appeared that they were very accommodative, flexible, caring, and honest guys. Our contact point was a person called Nir, who provided all the required information along with a carefully crafted itinerary for the trek and assigned his brother Santosh as a guide for us. If you recall, I have written a chapter earlier that was solely dedicated to him.

Now brace yourselves as I take you through our exploration of the actual trek. We were at the cusp of something truly adventurous and remarkable. Our enthusiasm mixed in with a bit of nerves was palpable. I thought it best to describe our journey day by day, so that you might feel as you

Our Tour Guide-Nir and Santosh

read, like as if you are right there with us, as we experienced the good, the bad and the ugly - all mixed into one delightful pot pourri of adventure.

We began our trek by walking through the entrance gate (that you see here) and registered at the Municipality counter. If you notice, there is a bust of a woman on either side of the gate. She is Pasang Lhamu, the first Nepali woman to ever climb Mount Everest.

Pasang Lhamu-1st Nepali woman to climb Mount Everest

Day 1 – Lukla to Phakding: From 2840m to 2610m (around 7.5kms)

We initially started our trek with a steady descent for almost four and a half hours. There were so many people, who had landed at Lukla Airport after three days of flight cancellations and were now heading to Phakding and onwards. Some of them went ahead to Namche Bazar, some stayed at Monjo, a small village between Phakding and Namche. Our stay was at Phakding, a decline in elevation by 230m. Our itinerary was prepared, keeping in mind that we were novices.

Our guide had taken all the required permits from the Khumbu Pasang Lhamu Rural Municipality ticket counter and we finally began our journey. The four and half-hour trek was really good. We did not find it so hard. In fact, it was scenic and overlooked the massive mountains in the background colored by giant green trees and the flowing Doodhkoshi river. The sound of the flowing river was so meditative that it lingered long after. There were small villages on the way along with a few small cafes for everyone to rest and rejuvenate. The weather was good, sunny, and warm. We had coffee at the Himalayan Sherpa Coffee, the world's highest coffee roaster, it was good and the view from there was simply amazing. We saw many Mani rocks (these are Tibetian inscriptions which have a mantra inscribed on them that reads – 'Om Mani Padme Hum'. It is said that when one encounters them one had to pass by them on their left in a clockwise direction because according to Buddhist beliefs that is how the universe spins), Mani walls, prayer flags, Mount Kongde, and Kusum Kanguru (a mountain that was 6300m high) during the walk from Lukla to Phakding.

The trail gradually ascended from Thadokoshi to Ghat and descended to Phakding for the final part. We reached our Lodge-Green village Guest house at around 1 pm.

This was our first day on the trek and needless to say, we were excited. Since it was a descent, we felt it was a fairly easy day, without knowing at the time that it would be the last time we would ever say something like that.

We were welcomed with hot lemon and honey tea, a staple drink on the entire trek which helped us feel refreshed. We then had lunch and rested for a while. At 4 pm we went hiking, to acclimatize ourselves with the weather. Santosh was a good task master. He made sure we did not rest much and used the time to warm up, as we would be missing our acclimatization day in Namche. It was indeed a hard climb but was necessary as this would help us during our walks in the future. We went to a monastery, that they call Gumba. It was my first time in a monastery and this time as well, we were lucky to have got to witness the prayer ceremony. We sat inside for around half an hour; the chanting of mantras and the rhythm was so meditative, peaceful, and inviting. They offered us some tea as well. There were around twenty-five to thirty students who stay there and learn. They study language, math, spirituality while they work in the monastery and visit the nearby village for shopping.

After our visit, we began our descent to our guest house, had dinner and slept. The lodge was good, and the food was delicious. Wifi was free, no cost to charge phones or power banks, free warm water to drink, but we had to pay 500 NPR if we had to take a hot shower. I dared myself that day and took a cold shower. It was not an attempt to save money but just to push myself to do something new and out of the ordinary.

After our dinner, we slept like babies. The feeling had started sinking in, that we were finally on the trek.

Namche Bazaar

Day 2 – Phakding to Namche Bazar: From 2610m to 3440m (around 10.5kms)

The next morning, we had our breakfast and left at around 8.45 am. Enroute we grabbed some banana bread from a bakery. We were told by numerous YouTubers that this would be one of the toughest walks and they were right. We stopped at Waterfall Hotel for a quick tea break and then lunch at Riverside Lodge and Restaurant. The lunch was delicious, simple dal, rice, potato curry, papad and pickle. This meal would need to give us enough strength to carry on for the rest of the day. There is a popular saying there doing the rounds – 'Daal Bhat Power, 24 hours.'

The entire trek varied from moderate to high in terms of difficulty levels. It involved steep climbs, stairs, and descents but the mantra was to go slow and steady. Due to the cloud cover, we missed our first chance to see Everest from one of the viewpoints. We met so many people on the way - locals, tourists, porters, and villagers and they all shared respect and warmth towards each other. No one was trying to show off or judge anyone, just because someone was slower than the rest. They all cheered and encouraged the others to carry on. It was wonderful to see such camaraderie among strangers. During our trek on that day, we also crossed a few hanging bridges.

It was quite an experience to walk across the picturesque hanging bridge with tall mountains towards the head and tail end of the bridge, a river on the right as well as on the left and some more mountains in the distance. The weather was beautiful, warm and sunny but all the peaks were covered by clouds, making it harder to look beyond. But we did get to see Thamserku and Ama Dablam on the way. There were so many waterfalls on the way, two of them were really big ones.

Two things were our constant companions throughout the trek- the presence of massive mountains and the musical sound of water from the flowing river.

There were so many cafes, and restaurants on the way, selling snacks, lunch, tea, water bottles etc. We also encountered porters, mules and jopke (a hybrid between a cow and a yak) carrying heavy loads. If you encounter them in a narrow space, we quickly learned that we needed to stand towards the side, ensuring that the load they were carrying did not push us. After we passed through the village of Monjo we made our way to the entry point of Sagarmatha National Park. It is here where all your climbing passes are checked and verified.

One of the many suspension bridges

They have a miniscule model of the mighty Himalayan ranges there, right near the ticket counter.

By 2 pm we were exhausted, we started taking more short breaks. We saw some tourists riding horses, as they found it challenging to walk. Especially after the last suspension bridge, the trek got a bit tougher. From there the path was sometimes very steep and zig zagged its way up. And that is when my brain popped in a couple of thoughts – 'Why Am I doing this? Can I go back from here?'. It was exhausting, to say the least.

If the second day was this hard, how would I manage the next eleven to twelve days. Even Kappiil and Gavin were struggling. Our porter was the fittest of the lot. He used to leave early, take a minimum number of stops and would reach the destination a couple of hours before us. Sometimes he would even come back to carry our back packs so we could walk faster. Today was extremely hard. By the end of it, we could not even feel our legs.

Finally, we reached Namche Bazar just around 5 pm. We had almost walked for eight hours and we went straight to Everest Bakery – the first café we saw on our way in, where we quickly consumed some tea and cake. Only after half an hour, were we in a position to appreciate this small but beautiful town, Namche Bazar. It sits at the bottom of a mountainous slope, with three to four storey white and blue buildings with blue tiles on top of them, this town was the last spot, wherein one could find ATMs, banks, money exchange stores and shops to buy any outdoor gear or winter clothing.

The town looked exactly like a painting. There were pubs, cafes, restaurants, pizza shops, bakeries, bars and other eateries. Usually, most people would spend two nights in Namche as the second day was meant for acclimatization. So, this was the best place for them to just unwind and have a good time before they head to EBC. Unfortunately, we had to skip the acclimatization, as we had already lost two days, due to the annoying flight cancellations. By this time, the high-altitude sickness symptoms started showing up, so one had to be very cautious and attentive to address them, without any further delay. Symptoms included headaches, nausea, vomiting, insomnia and reduced performance and coordination. Usually, the tour guide carried medication, but if symptoms persisted, it was best to descend immediately.

We stayed at the Yak Hotel. The owner who was a lady was very friendly. She was called Nima, which means Sunday. The room we got, was very basic, but after complaining a little, she moved us to an attached room, which also came with a complimentary hot shower which was a luxury from here onwards. Most of the guest houses, preferred that you ate there, so we had our dinner so as not to upset the owners. But before that, I must admit, that we did head out, to explore the place and had pizza at a place called Highcamp Pizza, I would recommend that everyone try their pizzas and pasta. At the Yak hotel, one could charge their phone for free but had to pay for Wi-Fi, which was around 500 NPR. Electricity, internet and hot showers were considered luxuries on the trek, especially in an area as high as Namche Bazar and upwards. So, one had to prioritize when and where to charge their phones and use Wi-Fi.

After our dinner, we slept like we had been beaten up, only to wake up nice and fresh the next morning for breakfast at 7.30 am. Before we went to bed, Gavin wanted to copy all the photos from Kappiil's phone to an SD card, he was trying his best to make optimum use of everyone's phone and his own camera as well. He was after all the official photographer of the group. But I guess, everyone was so tired that Kappiil surprisingly got upset and as a result the transfer of photos did not happen. It was so hard to keep calm when your body is that exhausted and all you want to do is rest and sleep. Only later we realised why Kappiil had behaved in that manner which I will tell you more about in the following chapter.

When I woke up the next morning and looked outside the window, the view was simply stunning. I could see the mountains in the distance, covered with snow and the sun was just peeking, slowly spreading its reddish orange radiance across the expanse of the mountains. It was simply beautiful. But I had no time to appreciate the beautiful canvas in front of me, as we had to leave for our next destination.

Day 3 – Namche Bazar to Deboche: From 3440m to 3830m. (around 12kms)

All three of us were feeling Ok, except for experiencing some mild headaches. I took a Crocin before I went to bed, and I was ok the next morning. Kappiil had some issues sleeping but he was fine too and Gavin was supercharged. We had our breakfast and left at around 8.45 am.

By then we had our routine set. We would reach our destination by around 4 pm or earlier, place our dinner order and rest. Once dinner was done, we were to place our breakfast order for the following day. Everything was meant to work by the clock. If we said, breakfast was at 7.30 am, it would be ready at 7.30 am, whether you were at the table or not. The same thing happened in the evening as well, usually the kitchen closed around 8–8.30 pm and everything was closed by 10 pm max, as everyone had to get up bright and early in the morning, to prepare breakfast for the tourists and hikers. You were offered a variety of dishes to choose from, for breakfast - sandwiches, pancakes, toast, eggs (scrambled or omelette), hash brown, or porridge. And finally, tea or coffee. I tried their Tibetian bread with jam once and found it to be heavy. Lunch options included Nepali thali (Rice, dal, potato curry, pickles, papad) or if you chose to, you could even order pizza, Thukpa, soup, stew, spring rolls, fried rice etc. All these places also offered non-vegetarian dishes as well. Considering all the meat was transported by either yak or mules, it could take days to reach its destination, Due to this, it was safer to stick to vegetarian options. And no doubt, the taste was amazing.

Nepali Thali

We were travelling to Deboche where we were in for a surprise. The walk started with a steep set of stairs and that was an indication of what one could expect ahead. After that climb, the path was mostly straight for a while. We stopped for lunch at Zambala Lodge and Restaurant in a place called Phunki Thanga. I swapped my rice with roti as I had had enough rice by then.

Ever since we landed in Kathmandu, Kappiil had been entertaining us and the other tourists with his amazing soulful voice. And he continued doing so on the trek as well. We were constantly entertained at the different places where we had lunch, during overnight stays or even at the places where we had tea. Here too, while we were waiting for our lunch, Kappiil started singing. The owner/manager liked it and started encouraging us. He had two young daughters and their father jokingly said that he wanted us to take his girls to Australia with us, but they did not have their passports.

Again, the food was very well made. The path that we took passed around ridges and then descended into the valley to again meet the Doodhkoshi river. From here on, the trail headed back up through the forest and into a vast display of Rhododendron bushes…although in September they were not in bloom…or else it would have been a sight to behold! The scenery was beautiful. By now the tall trees were gone and were replaced by shorter trees. As a result, we could see more mountains covered with snow. We reached Thyangboche at around 3.30 pm. Since we were so tired, we decided to have some refreshments which was cake and tea at Tashi Delek Lodge and Restaurant. We noticed that there was a monastery there in front of the cafe. This is the biggest monastery in the Khumbu region apparently. Since we had already gone to one in Phakding, we decided to skip visiting that one.

From there we headed down to Deboche, which was around forty to forty-five minute's walk. Finally, after eight long hours we reached Deboche, it was a bit cold and cloudy when we reached. But the entire trek was very scenic with some beautiful views and stupas on the way. On that day too, we noticed so many porters carrying luggage to the next town. Life was so hard on the mountains. They got paid as per the weight they carried. Some of them were carrying around ninety to ninety-five kgs, walking for two to three days and they got finally paid around 70 or 75 NPR per kg, was what I was given to understand. It was too little an amount for so much of a strain on their physical being was what I felt but there was nothing to be done about it. The other mode of transport were yaks or mules. We saw so many on the way, carrying cylinders and essential items.

Porters carrying stuff weighing easily around 80 to 90kgs.

The place we stayed in Deboche were full of trekkers. There was a Russian group of eleven people, a group from UK with nine of them and the three of us, amongst others. And that was where I met Steve from UK. There was a couple from Bulgaria. The husband was a photographer. Since he wanted to capture the night view and sunrise, they were trekking in the night, just by themselves without a guide, or a porter. They were to start their trek to Dingboche in the night at around 12–12.30 am, hoping to reach by around 7 am. I was amazed by how daring and enthusiastic people could be. We met them again in Gorakshep and in Lukla, towards the end of the trip.

It was cold, so I had decided to sit in the dining area. Kappiil took some rest and Gavin was busy editing and transferring photos from the trek. In Deboche and in any other place beyond this point, they switched on heaters in the evening as it got chillingly cold. The fuel for the heater was mainly yak poo. So, most of the people, usually gathered around in the evening in the dining area to take advantage of the heat. Some played cards, some discussed their day or made friends with others. The rooms did not have any charging points, but you could charge your phone at the reception/ kitchen counter. The cost to charge a power bank was 500 NPR. By that point, I did not even care to enquire about a hot shower, as I had taken one the day before. The lodge had common toilets which were pretty decent. Most of the places had both western toilets and squat toilets, also commonly referred to as Indian toilets. There were no toilet paper rolls available though. Either you had to carry your own or go to some place that might have a jet spray or just use a bucket full of water and a jug. No flush as well, you would have to manually clear your mess with the help of a bucket of water.

Day 4 – Deboche to Dingboche:- From 3830m to 4360m (around 10 kms)

It rained heavily overnight in Deboche, so I was a bit worried about the weather the following day and how the path we had to take would be affected by it. Following our ritual every day, we left a little early at 7.30 am after having breakfast at Deboche. It was a nice and comparatively easy walk on that day. The day was bright and sunny, and the view kept getting better and better. The paths were getting narrower by then. We were now above the tree line. We had lunch at Hilltop Lodge in Somare.

We reached Dingboche at around 3.30 pm, after around seven or eight hours of trekking continuously. It was still sunny outside. I decided to take advantage of the heat and wash my clothes at that point which was a luxury on the trek. Since we would be staying there for two nights, tomorrow being an acclimatization day, I thought it would be a great idea. They did have laundry service in the guest house, but they charged us per item – a pair of socks was 150 NPR, tee-shirts were 300 and so on. So, I washed a few of my clothes myself and put them on the clothesline. An hour later, it got cloudy, and it stayed that way, until the next evening. But I did manage to dry some of them near the heater.

In the evening, while Kappiil and Gavin were resting in the room, I decided to stay in the dining area and make some friends. One of the guides from another group taught me a card game, widely played in Nepal. The Bulgarians were also there. They left at night from Deboche and managed to dodge the rains.

When Kappiil entered the dining area, just before dinner, we had a musical evening. He sang and then everyone had to sing one song in their language. The uncle from Myanmar was sportive enough to sing a song for us and so did the Brazilians. A girl from Calcutta, India also joined and then a guide from Nepal sang my favourite Nepali song-

Resham Firiri, Resham Firiri

Udera Jaau ki, danda maa Bhanjyang

Resham Firiri….!

Resham Firiri is a popular Nepali song that demonstrates the cultural values and unbeatable natural spectrum that draws immense attention to Nepal. It is also a popular trekking song of Nepal.

My heart is fluttering like silk in the wind

I cannot decide whether to fly or sit on the hilltop.

Since the next day was a rest day or an acclimatization day, we were relaxed and decided to sleep in. I went for a small walk in the evening, just to see the village. I also took a hot water shower; I paid 800 NPR for it. This would be my last shower for the next five days. By then it was dark and cold. Most of the tourists were in their guest houses and some locals were going back to their homes. After I came back, we had our dinner and went to bed, got up at around 8.30 am. Phone charging was a free service at this hotel, but to charge your power bank you had to pay 1000 NPR. A bottle of warm drinking water cost 500 NPR. Wi-Fi was not working since the day before. We were told the same thing when we were in Deboche. The network was down. But they also had Starlink Wi-Fi which was a different service provider. The cost was 1500 NPR for 24 hours. Since, I had no urgency, I decided not to opt for it. The place had common toilets which were clean but again had no toilet rolls. The sink was outside without any soap.

In every town there were several lodges. When we booked Ghumnajaao's services, they took care of booking all the places enroute. Breakfast, lunch, and dinner was included and so was sightseeing in Kathmandu. Pickup and drop off was also part of the package and the hotel stay in Kathmandu as well. Based on one's budget, one could choose where to stay and what facilities to avail, though on the trek the options were very limited.

Day 5 – Acclimatization day in Dingboche.

The next morning, I had a mild headache, but I was still feeling Ok. I was taking a Crocin almost every day, so I had no issues that far. Kappiil was still tired, he had issues sleeping for the past two nights so he decided to take some rest. Gavin and I were up for another hike. The reason to have an acclimatization day is to get yourself accustomed to the weather and the altitude. So, you hike higher and sleep lesser. People usually, hike up to a certain height in the morning, come back for lunch and then rest in the afternoon until late evening. So, we left at around 10.30 am for another hike. There were around seven points in all. I stopped at point three and decided to come back, hoping to rest and write a bit.

Mr. Author

Gavin and our guide decided to go further, so they went ahead(upwards). I had my lunch and got busy writing about the trek. It was 4 pm and we realised that the guys were still not back from their hike. Since there was no phone network, I was unable to contact them. Kappiil and I were worried by then, since both of them had not had their lunch nor were they carrying enough supplies. (water and snacks). Our guide finally came back by 4.30 pm. Apparently ambitious Gavin had gone all the way up to the last point, as he was very keen to achieve that, in his enthusiasm not realising that it could be dangerous.

By the time he started descending, he had already run out of water, snickers, and stamina. So, we had to send our porter to help him get back to the lodge, it was like a mini rescue mission. Thankfully, he was alright, just drained, and tired. He told us that he had the best view and experience that far, in being able to reach close to 5000m, and it was rewarding for sure. In general Gavin was very energetic throughout the trek. He was always ahead of us, sprinting, running and walking fast. I wanted to be like him to be honest. How could he have that much energy and I could not. But eventually I would catch up with him and laugh about it.

In the evening Kappiil had promised to make Indian style masala chai and managed to gain entry into the kitchen. That was the best tea I have had to date.

Day 6 – Dingboche to Lobuche: – From 4360m to 4930m (around 8.5 kms)

One of the Stupas

On this day, we were told that it would be a flat walk except for the last two hours, where it would get difficult and exhausting, but nothing like Phakding to Namche. Honestly, every day until that point, I felt like each day was harder than the last. The day was beautiful, bright, and sunny. There were so many people on the way, some we had already met and some completely unknown faces. That is where we met the Arizona family from my previous story, who were on vacation for fourteen months (I was so jealous). It was a nice walk, though Kappiil and Gavin were struggling a bit, Gavin off course, because of his heroics, the previous day.

The small trees were soon replaced by shrubs. We started seeing mountain goats and yaks frequently. The trek continued like this until Thukla, where we had lunch. We had to cross a river to get to the other side and climb up to have our lunch. This river is basically at the other end of Khumbu glacier, which we would see and walk on tomorrow. The trail in this section is the steepest and only got harder with the increased elevation. Climbing the trail to Dugla Pass did not get any easier, due to its sharp incline and low oxygen levels. And that anxious feeling kicked in again. 'Why am I doing this?' Every step I took made me think and doubt my decision to ever have wanted to attempt this trek.

'What was I trying to achieve? What was I trying to prove and to whom?'

But deep down in my heart, I knew that I had to. Especially, after what I went through in the last few years, I wanted to challenge myself. Somewhere I took it as a penance and to liberate myself from the situation I was in for the last three to four years. That is what fuelled me and I marched on to the next destination.

As I said earlier there was a place, just after Thukla, where there were several stone monuments that were erected in memory of those trekkers who lost their lives trekking. It was a place where they were fondly remembered. It served as a reminder, to all of us, that one could not conquer mother nature all the time, no matter, if you were doing it for the first time or the seventh, just like Don Cash did. Looking at that site and with sober feelings, we reached Lobuche at around 4 pm where it was so cold. The temperature was around three degrees which was a sudden change in the weather and the view.

We stayed at Hotel National Park that had very basic facilities. Common toilets without toilet rolls again, the wash basin was outside in the cold. We were using Gavin's power bank to charge our phones, as most of the guest houses did not have charging points in the rooms. The cost to charge the power bank was 1200 NPR and 500 NPR per litre to drink hot water. We were also carrying water purifier tablets. It is recommended to have those. You just add a tablet to your water bottle and let it settle for half an hour to make the water potable. Since we had to leave early the next morning, we had early dinner and slept at around 8.30 pm to prepare ourselves for the next day.

CHAPTER 10
D DAY

Everest Base Camp @ 5364m. A proud moment for all of us

Day 7 – Lobuche to EBC Via Gorakshep: – From 4930m to 5364m (Around 8kms)

The most anticipated day was finally here.

After walking for the last six days, we would finally be at the EBC today. Usually, trekkers follow the same itinerary. They leave early in the morning from Lobuche, they have their breakfast and an early lunch at Gorakshep and reach EBC by lunch time. They spend some time there and get back to Gorakshep for an overnight stay. We left at around 5.30 am, when it was still dark and cold. We had our breakfast packed for us to eat on the way. There were already people on the trail ahead of us. It almost looked like a long queue of people heading to a pilgrimage site. The only thing in everyone's mind was, the Everest Base Camp. Watching the sunrise at around 5000m was a different experience altogether. It was so fresh in the morning, though it was cold, but very pleasant. As the sun was rising, slowly the snow-capped mountain tops began to turn red. I had never seen such a beautiful sight in my life, ever. It was so beautiful that I was hoping that I could stay there forever. But today, we were heading to our destination, I had been dreaming about, for the last seven to eight years. So, we started our walk, joined by so many other like-minded people.

We were surrounded by the giants – the Pobuche (6119m), the Pumori (7165m) and others. Looking at those giants, up close was a surreal experience for me. And they were still 1500m shorter than the highest mountain on earth. So, imagine, how tall the Everest would be. I felt so tiny in front of those mountains. Their vastness made me think of the way we humans behave. We were just a tiny speck in front of mother nature, the universe and still we behaved as if the world would not go on without us. It really helped put things in perspective while I was up there.

Long queue heading to Gorakshep

Back to reality for now. Today's trek was very beautiful and unique, that involved crossing a lot of loose rock, boulder fields and glacial moraine and not to mention, another tough walking day. It was challenging to say the least, to walk on the glacier and on the loose rocks. It was very different to the previous day's journey. It was definitely more tiring. And we had to walk like that for nearly eight to nine hours today. The up and down trail into Gorak Shep took approximately three to three and a half hours. So, we were aiming to be there between 9 and 9.30 am, have an early lunch and then start walking to EBC, which could take another two and a half to three hours.

The view was astonishing, though the path was very rough, but everyone's eyes were trained on the horizon in trying to capture the beauty that was all around. We were walking slowly but steadily. Kappiil and Gavin, both were struggling today, but the incentive to be at the EBC was what kept their spirits high. After an hour we had our breakfast and started walking again. Since everyone started early from Lobuche, they packed their breakfast so that they could eat on the way in order to save time. The guys at the lodge had done an awesome job on that front. We reached Gorakshep at around 11 am, we were a bit behind schedule, but it was still nice and sunny, so we were very hopeful to have good weather when we finally reached EBC.

We had lunch at the Himalaya Lodge & Restaurant, that is where we would be spending our night. Considering Kappiil and Gavin needed some rest, we spent some extra time there. The rooms were basic as usual, the toilets were on the ground floor and were very dirty. There we could find only the squatting types. There were two outside as well and both were competing for first place in being the dirtiest. Only a day later, when we were headed back, did I come to know that there were western and clean toilets upstairs, but it was too late by then.

The Wi-Fi was again charged at 1500 NPR and the cost to charge the power bank was now 2500 NPR. A toilet roll would cost around 500 NPR. While exploring the lodge, I saw the statue of Shivaji Maharaj. Chhatrapati Shivaji Maharaj was a 17th-century Indian ruler who founded the Maratha Empire by challenging the Mughal Empire through guerrilla warfare and strategic alliances. Those from India and especially from Maharashtra and neighbouring states, can relate to that part. This statue was installed in 2012 by Giripremi, Pune, India in collaboration with the Everest Summiteers Association, it personally was a very proud moment for me to have seen that statue there.

We were exhausted by then. And Kappiil and Gavin were literally struggling. They took a power nap just after lunch. After some deliberation, we decided to leave at around 1 pm for EBC. Ideally, it should not have taken more than two and half hours to get there, but again we decided to go slow. The path was narrow and slippery. Since it was already late, there were not many people walking towards EBC, but we saw many coming back from EBC, with a sense of achievement, cheering us and encouraging us. Some tourists chose to take a horse ride from Gorakshep to EBC and back which costed around USD $100–$120.

The walk started on plain ground and then there were lots of ups and downs. At some point, we were also walking on the glacier. It was hard, throughout. We could hear the cracking noise from within the glacier, sometimes we heard

Chattrapati Shivaji Maharaj

a rumbling noise from a mountain somewhere, far from us. But my excitement level was at its peak. This was what we had been preparing ourselves for, since the last eight to nine months. We were so close to achieving one of the items on our bucket list. And we were getting there....slowly.....one step at a time, enjoying the view and congratulating fellow travellers who were returning.

Finally, we reached the Base Camp at around 4 pm. Unfortunately, the weather turned bad by then and became cold. White clouds had now covered all the mountains. There were very few people at the site. A group from the UK, whom we met multiple times before, another small group from Malaysia, we had met them, first in Ramechhap when our flight had gotten cancelled and a couple more. We spent around half an hour, clicking some pictures and talking to others. It is very hard for me to express my feelings now on paper, to convey how I felt back then when I was there.

It was a bag of mixed emotions for sure. There was an overwhelming sense of pride and awe, realizing I was in the shadow of the world's tallest peak, a place everyone had heard of, but very few had a chance to see in person. At the same time, a quiet humility settled in, as I reflected on the immense effort it took to get there and the sheer power of nature surrounding me. It was both exhilarating and grounding—a reminder of how small we were in the face of such grandeur, yet how capable we were when we dared to dream. The feelings swirling inside me at that moment, left me with a deep sense of gratitude and wonder.

It would be remiss of me if I did not take a moment to thanks Santosh, our very able tour guide, Dig Bahadur, our strong porter and Nir from Gumnajaau for their help and care.

And it goes without saying that I would like to thank God for giving us the strength and wisdom to have kept us motivated and grounded all the time that we were there.

With happy faces and a heavy heart, we headed back to Gorakshep. It took two and a half hours to get back to Gorakshep. We were happy because we had finally done it and we felt heavy because the most exciting part of the trip was over and now, we had to return....to our lives and to reality.

As per our original plan, we are supposed to go to Gokyo from EBC. Gokyo is beautiful, challenging and totally worth it, so we had decided, that we would do both, while we were there. The next day's plan was to get up early in the morning to climb Kala Patthar and then head to Zhongla, for our onward journey. We had dinner and slept by 9 pm that night, anticipating an early start.

But things changed dramatically, overnight. Stay tuned for what happened next......

It's not the mountains we conquer but ourselves – Sir Edmund Hillary.

CHAPTER 11

CLIMAX

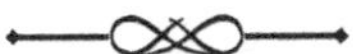

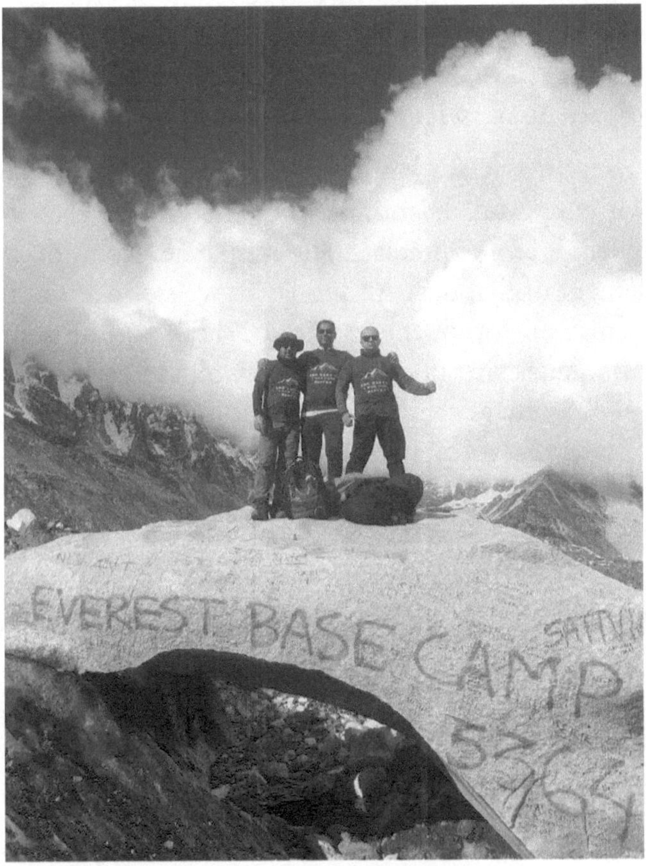

People won't see your struggle;
they will only see your success.

23rd of Sept:

All of us were incredibly happy, satisfied, and proud of our achievement. We had been preparing and practicing for almost eight to nine months for the Everest Base Camp and had done everything that was required. We had been watching YouTube videos to understand what the trek looked like, what we needed to pack, what we could skip packing, how to prepare ourselves, etc.

From the day we landed in Lukla and embarked on our trek, we congratulated ourselves at the end of each day, to acknowledge and appreciate our resilience, strength and the achievement of that day. And today as we stood at the Everest Base Camp, on top of the iconic rock, taking our photos, all those moments came flooding into my mind like an avalanche. But we all knew at that time that the road to that point was definitely not easy, for any of us.

I do not only refer to the preparation for the trek but everything else as well, until the day we completed the trek. It brought back memories of the day we decided to do this or probably even a little before that reminding us that nothing was ever easy. Kappiil had his own issues that he was dealing with and Gavin had his. You already know mine. So, for the three of us, it was not just any achievement but an extremely important milestone in our lives.

Even though Kappiil had hiked in New Zealand and was aware of what a hike typically involved, the last few years had been very difficult for him. In the years leading up to Covid and especially during the pandemic, he found himself feeling less motivated and engaged with his usual activities. He had once been an avid table tennis player and never skipped his daily walks, even in the rain. However, over the last three to four years, his routine has become more sedentary, with most evenings spent on the couch and weekends absorbed in television. His walks are now mostly limited to short trips, like those from the car park to his office or the nearest shopping centre. Even after booking our tickets, mentally and emotionally, he was still not ready to start practicing, till about two months later.

Though I did not know Gavin so well before the trek, to know much about him, I was aware that he had his own struggles as well. Back in Melbourne, he would miss some of the practices and almost pulled out from the trek a month before our flight. When he had initially landed in Kathmandu, he still seemed a little preoccupied due to the weight of his emotions from everything he was going through. But slowly as we advanced through the trek, I could see that the weight from his shoulder lifted a bit and he seemed more in tune with nature. Thankfully it stayed that way for most part of the trek.

On the way back to Gorakshep, I had used the time to reflect on everything, especially the last seven to eight days. Every day we had walked, for almost six to eight hours on an average, on a difficult trek, at high altitude, with low oxygen levels. This was not only physically demanding but it took a toll on everyone, mentally and emotionally as well. By God's grace, everything went as planned and none of us had any major health issues, until then.

But we were wrong. It was brewing under the surface which we failed to notice and address at the correct time.

We all had made it to the Base Camp, but how? Or how well?

Let us go back in time to the point when we were in Namche Bazar. I guess, that was where it all started to go down although we had no inkling at the time. Kappiil could not sleep well, he had his dinner and went to bed but had a disturbed sleep. The next day when he got up, he felt fine, he looked fresh and we started walking to Deboche. The same thing happened in Deboche and then in Dingboche as well. He could not sleep for three nights in a row. When we reached Dingboche, he was exhausted. He slept all evening and the next day as well, which was an acclimatization day. He had very little food in his stomach. We went for a short walk in the evening on the second day in Dingboche. Whatever energy he had left within him was completely drained out the next day, when we walked from Dingboche to Lobuche. Four nights without enough sleep, barely any food, low oxygen levels and change in altitude and atmosphere was making it more and more difficult for him. His mind wanted to continue and be at the Base Camp, but his body wanted to go back, to descend, so it could recover. He declined to get on a horse from Lobuche to EBC to complete his journey. He wanted to walk, that is what he had signed up for.

At the same time, Gavin had developed some symptoms of his own. He took the acclimatizing in Dingboche literally and went all the way up, only to get exhausted on the way back, so much so that he never recovered from it, even after reaching Melbourne. He had a mild fever in Dingboche, but thankfully he was eating well. I think that was the main difference between the two of them. The trek from Dingboche to Lobuche was not that difficult, except the last two hours, where again they both were slow and took their time, took frequent breaks and we finally reached Lobuche. It was cold in Lobuche that night and those two struggled to sleep again.

But the next day, we left early at 5.30 am, the plan was to be at Gorakshep by 9 am and then to EBC by around 1 pm. It was a hard and difficult trek, all the way to EBC.

While the fight continued between the mind and the body, we somehow reached Gorakshep at around 11 am, two hours later than we had initially targeted. After lunch, they both went to bed, slept for an hour or so. By then we were contemplating whether to cancel going to EBC that afternoon and review the situation the next day. Oxygen levels were just under sixty for both of them. But then next day we were to go to Kala Patther and then to Zhongla, so it would be another hectic day for all of us. Even if we cancelled Kala Patther and did EBC and Zhongla, it would still be a challenging ask. We had even wondered if at that point we should leave Kappiil behind and continue our trek to EBC, without him? We were in a bit of a quandary for sure.

Eventually, we agreed to continue and headed to EBC the same day.

Halfway to EBC, Kappiil realised that he could not continue anymore. He could not take one more step. Finally, on the way to the base camp from Gorakshep, we convinced him to ride a horse to the base camp and back to Gorakshep. That was how he reached EBC, took some photos and rode back to Gorakshep. Even though Gavin was struggling he pushed himself and walked with us to EBC and back to Gorakshep. Once we were back, we checked their oxygen levels, and it had dropped to 55, which was alarming and needed immediate attention. At least Gavin was eating, so he was in better shape than Kappiil, but nevertheless the situation was alarming. It was 7.30 pm, the weather was bad, so we had to wait until next day morning to arrange a helicopter for medical evacuation. It was now certain that Kappiil could not continue the trek. So, while he was sleeping, we decided to send him back to Kathmandu, the next morning and to continue our trek to Zhongla but possibly skip Kala Patthar.

It was freezing in Gorakshep. Thankfully, there was no medical emergency that night, but it felt like a ticking time bomb, which could have exploded at any time. In the morning when we had checked Kappiil's oxygen level, we found that it was still around sixty, which was not a good sign and Gavin's was still under fifty-five, which was still worrisome. We were at the breakfast table that morning, planning our next move. Considering we had two out of three of us struggling to walk and cope with the altitude, the option was to cancel Gokyo and walk back the normal way. Or send Kappiil and Gavin by horseback to Lobuche/Pheriche and we walk back and then review the situation. But we were sure at the time that even that was not doable. We ran the risk of them collapsing from the horse, which was not a safe option.

Rescue Helicopter

Finally, we decided to send both of them back to Kathmandu. All the excitement, happiness, sense of achievement now turned into worry and a feeling of helplessness kicked in. But we knew, that was the best thing to do. There was no way, that the two of them could have survived another night in Gorakshep.

Things changed so quickly once we made that decision. Our guide spoke to the guest house manager, who in turn arranged a rescue helicopter. Thankfully, they both had insurance and high-altitude rescue cover. The helicopter arrived in half an hour. We packed everything, escorted them to the helicopter and loaded their bags in. Within the next ten mins, they were flown to Kathmandu.

That left me behind in Gorakshep with our guide and porter. Seeing my friends being medically evacuated by helicopter was a harrowing experience. My heart raced with fear and anxiety, unsure of their condition and hoping for the best. I felt a profound sense of helplessness, wishing there was something more I could do. Amidst the chaos, there was also a glimmer of relief and gratitude for the swift and professional response of the rescue team. The sight of the helicopter taking off with my friends was both terrifying and reassuring, knowing they were in capable hands. It was an emotional rollercoaster and the impact of that moment will stay with me for a long time. They were struggling by then but once in Kathmandu and in the hospital with good care and medication, they would soon start to feel better.

They were kept in the hospital for twenty-four hours in Kathmandu under medication and observation. They were then discharged and were resting in the hotel, for the next two to three days. Though the decision to send them back was accurate and timely, it happened so quickly that it took a while for me to acknowledge and accept the reality that, I would be walking back alone, without them. My guide had offered me the option to fly back with them as a companion. But I had declined. Thankfully I was physically able to walk back and I found it reassuring to stick to the plan. At that point, I had a compelling reason to walk, I was not only walking for myself, but I was doing it for the team, for them, in their absence. I obviously, did not want to do the Gokyo trail without them so I decided to walk back the normal route.

If you listen to your body when it whispers....
you won't have to hear it scream.

And that is a lesson we all learned a little late. Both of them did not listen to the whispers of their body and the result was a medical evacuation, which none of us had even imagined. Especially in the mountains, one must always listen to their body and not their mind. Thankfully, they both managed to reach Base Camp. Though I had witnessed their struggle and weakness over the last few days, it was still hard for me to comprehend, what they must have gone through internally, while they were walking and especially when they were airlifted. So, hats off to both for making it to the Base Camp.

Many trekkers experience high-altitude sickness—some push through to reach base camp, while others turn back to Namche or even return to Kathmandu. However, fewer than five percent require medical evacuation, with Kappiil and Gavin among them—a rare distinction, though not one to boast about.

The Photo op at the Base Camp was the success that everyone saw, but most of them never saw the struggle behind it.

CHAPTER 12
THE RETURN

Pheriche on the 25th of Sept Morning

With the two of them safely in Kathmandu I had the luxury of having the guide and the porter just to myself. It was the 24th of Sept and my flight from Lukla to Kathmandu was on the 29th. Santosh suggested that we explore the small villages on the way back, take a detour, spend some time seeing different places and different people. I willingly accepted his idea as I still had five days to get back, where normally it took three. So, we decided to push ourselves and started walking back.

We had our lunch and left Gorakshep at around 12 pm and reached Thukla at 4 pm. It was the same route we took on the way to EBC, so there was nothing new or unfamiliar, the only difference was that we were now descending and losing altitude and I was missing my travel buddies. There was still some daylight, so we continued and reached Pheriche at around 6.30 pm. It was dark and started drizzling. We stayed at Pumori Lodge. I was tired, as it has been a hectic and very emotional day for all of us. So, we had our dinner at around 8 pm and went to bed straight away. I could not sleep properly in Gorakshep, the previous night. It was freezing, even though I had slept inside a sleeping bag, it was barely enough. I did not find it very comfortable and it was also my first time sleeping in one. I was hoping to get a good night's rest, but I had no luck. I spent the night tossing and turning while noticing that it rained and snowed overnight.

25th of Sept:

We got up early the next morning, had breakfast and left at 7 am. The weather had cleared out and it was a beautiful sunny day, we encountered many people, on the way, walking back to Namche Bazar. But my guide had a different plan. We took a detour and went to Pangboche first via Somare and then to Phortse. The idea was to cover as much ground as possible on that day, so we could visit another small village the next day, near Namche Bazar and then head to Namche. We took small breaks in between and reached Pangboche at around 10 am. This was just after I met Pavin, the cute little boy from my earlier story.

This village had a monastery which was originally built in the 16th century but was destroyed by massive avalanches during the winter season and later rebuilt in 1667 AD. Lama Sangwa Dorje, the sixth reincarnation of Lama Chhagna Dorje and the king of the Khumbu region built the Pangboche Monastery. Known as "The Flying Lama" for his power to fly in the Khumbu area, he was a powerful monk. According to legend, a Yeti helped him by preparing food and water while he meditated in the nearby Taboche Cave. One day, the Yeti could not return due to a massive snowfall and was later found dead when the snow melted. Lama Sangwa Dorje brought the Yeti's skull and hand back to the monastery, where they remain to this day (see the pics below). After spending some time in the Monastery, we left for Phortse.

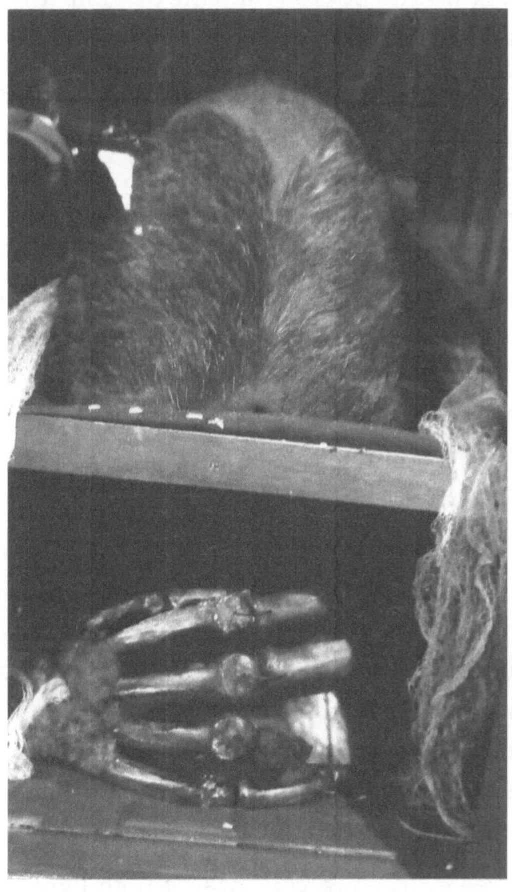

Yeti's Skull and Hand from the Monastery

The entire route was very scenic with tall mountains, lots of slopes and inclines, numerous staircases to climb up and down, steep hills. It was a tiring journey. The funniest part was that even my guide was taking this route for the first time, so he had no idea how long we would be walking for until we reached Phortse. I was frustrated, tired and angry. And I still could not see any sign of any village. Though from Pheriche to Phortse the elevation dropped from 4371m to 3840m, but the ascent was around 860m while the descent was only 370m, making it a difficult trek.

Finally, we reached Phortse at around 1.30 pm. This was a sherpa town and usually, the summiteers used this town and route to bypass the crowd to get to EBC. I was lucky enough to have met a sherpa here who had climbed Mount Everest twice. We had lunch and indulged in a bit of chit chat before we left town at around 3.30 pm. We had to walk for another three hours to get to another village, where we would be spending the night. It started pouring down, the moment we left the village. The trek was getting harder and harder and the rain was making it even worse.

After eleven hours of walking, we reached Mongla, a tiny place, where we would be sleeping that night. It was on a hilltop and obviously it was cold. The heater inside was not working. I had honey ginger and lemon tea as I sat in the dining area until dinner was served at around 8 pm. I took off to bed straight after. It was a basic place, more of a snacking place than meant for an overnight stay. But we had no energy left and the next town was another two and half hours away. That was why Santosh had decided to stay there.

The three of us were very tired which I am sure you can imagine based on how difficult the trek was and especially so when your guide and porter were tired too. Santosh was in my room and he dozed off, literally, in five minutes. it was just too cold for me; I tried sleeping inside the sleeping bag but could not. I got out of the bag, took the blanket and the sleeping bag on top of it and still found it to be too cold and uncomfortable. I went out at around 9.30 pm to see if I could grab another blanket, but everything outside was dark, freezing, and quiet. I guess, I was the only one awake at that time. So, I had to reluctantly go back and rearrange my sleeping bag. Somehow, I survived that night in that freezing cold and was eagerly waiting for sunrise.

26th of Sept:

Though I just wanted to do nothing, I thought it best to rest in Namche rather than here, in Mongla. It was still raining; the mountains were covered with clouds, but we decided to have our breakfast and leave for Namche. The manager at Mongla - Shiva, was a humble guy. We spoke about the seasonality of the business; the hardship small businesses face and about the caste system in Nepal. Shiva spoke a different dialect than my guide, Santosh. So, he explained to me that language was linked with caste. Rai people speak differently to Magars and to Kshatriyas. You could identify one's caste, based on what language they spoke, which was very different to India, where people belonging to different castes spoke the same language, based on the region they lived in and their mother tongue.

I loved understanding different cultures, their beliefs, and their way of life through the people I had met. The one thing I had noticed, in Kathmandu/Nepal was that no matter what one's caste was, no matter what their religion, or profession was, or if they were a Sherpa, a porter or a guide or a restauranteur, they all were so focussed on serving tourists and serving them well. They might have their internal differences and hierarchy, but they understood very well that their economy ran on tourism and they made sure, to keep tourists happy and satisfied. I found them to be very honest people.

I was still tired from the eleven hours walk yesterday, so we decided to skip visiting any other village and headed straight to Namche Bazar. It was mostly downhill from there and we reached Namche at 2 pm. We went straight to Yak Hotel, the same place where we had stayed, when we were at Namche last time. This time again, I got the attached bathroom, which meant a complimentary hot shower. But just the feeling of me being back in Namche, made me feel like I was back in civilisation. I took a shower, after five days and it felt like that glorious hot water washed away all the fatigue in my bones. We went out to explore Namche, we could not do that the last time we were there. It was such a beautiful town. It was like a mini city, with its pubs, Bars, ATM's, cafes, bakeries, outdoor clothing shops and so much more. Namche also has a few schools and hostels. Kids from the surrounding villages stay in the hostel and study in Namche.

I decided to take Santosh out to lunch, just to thank him for sticking around, for taking care of us including myself during the last three days. His intention to show me a different side of Khumbu region was very genuine. I could not thank him enough for all the care, support and the things I had learned from him. We had some heart-to-heart conversations enroute, since it was just the two of us during the last three days and would be for the next three days as well. We had pizza and lasagna at High camp Pizza and then went to Namche Bakery and had chocolate cake, which according to me are one of the best cakes I have had in a while. Though it was still raining, we walked around, looked at some shops and then went back to our guest house. Since it had been raining for the last two days, there were not many people in the guest house. I had dinner and finally had a sound sleep that night.

27th of Sept:

After having breakfast the next day, we left for Phakding. The rain had not stopped yet, but we had to continue our journey in the rain. I had a flight to catch on the 29th from Lukla. It was a nice but tiring walk of around six to seven hours and reached Phakding at around 2 pm. The view that we had enjoyed on the trail, on the way to EBC, was now covered in dense fog. By then, I was missing my other two friends a lot. They were doing fine in Kathmandu. But we had walked the same path a few days ago, stayed at the same places, in the same room, and had breakfast, lunch and dinner together. We had shared laughter and hard times together. But here I was, walking back just by myself for the last four days and would continue for another two, until I was with them again. In Phakding, we stayed at the same place, Green Village Guest House. The staff were very pleased to see me again and expressed that they did miss Kappiil and Gavin. We met a couple from Italy. They had arrived the day before and were waiting for the rain to stop, to continue their journey to EBC. Sadly, they had to wait for two more days until the weather was clear.

Views are covered with Clouds and dense Fog

28th of Sept:

The next day when we started our final leg from Phakding to Lukla, it was still raining. That was when we realised that we had not seen any people coming from the other side, for the last two days which was not good news. That meant that flights were not operating, which also meant, that there would be hordes of people stuck in Lukla who could not fly to Kathmandu. We reached Lukla at 1 pm, it was a short three and a half hour walk in the rain. Walking in the rains for the last four days, my waterproof jacket, shoes and pants had finally given up on me and could no longer protect me anymore. I was completely drenched when we had reached our destination the previous day and that day as well.

We went straight to our guest house, where we had our breakfast when we first landed in Lukla. Due to heavy rains, the phone network and internet was down, so we had no clue what was going on. All we knew was that flights were cancelled for the last three days. I was hopeful that the rain would stop overnight and we would be able to take the flight the next day. I spent that afternoon, talking to other travellers, listening to their stories.

Later I came to know that from 26th to 28th September 2024, Nepal was struck by exceptional late monsoon rainfall, inducing landslides and flooding across a wide swathe of the country. News reports indicate that the official loss of life was about 217 people, with a further 28 people that were still listed as missing. Another 142 people were injured.

While I had walked in the rain on all those days, I had no idea, that the weather had created such devastation in the rest of Nepal. I was thankful to God that I was still able to walk back to Lukla, without any issues.

Back in Lukla, I met one of our friends from Bangladesh with whom we had spent two days in Ramechhap, when our incoming flights had gotten cancelled. We spent the evening together, said good night, hoping we would see each other the next day at the airport. Luckily, the weather started clearing up.

29th of Sept:

My flight got rescheduled to 11 am from 8 am, which was expected, considering there was a fair bit of backlog to clear. My original flight ticket was from Lukla to Ramechhap and then I had a five-hour road trip to Kathmandu. But as per the news report, the roads to Kathmandu were closed due to a landslide, so I was still unsure about my travel plans.

The next day when we went to the airport, it was utter chaos. Though some of the flights had already taken off that morning to Ramechhap, there were still at least two hundred-and fifty-people at the airport waiting for their turn. It was a small airport; the flights were even smaller – an 18-seater. I met that Bulgarian couple who were stranded for the last four days. Knowing the condition of the roads, they wanted to fly to Kathmandu instead of Ramechhap, which was a fair ask. Thankfully the flights were still operating, and they were clearing the backlog speedily. Unfortunately, by the time my turn came, the weather changed, it became cloudy again and they had to stop operations. I went back to the guest house again. Lukla is a tiny place with just one main street so it literally took ten mins to walk from one end to the other. We did two rounds and still had an entire evening left to ourselves. We did some window shopping, had dinner, and went to bed.

Those, who have never been to Lukla or Ramechhap, this could be the most frustrating thing. The airport does not have any digital display boards to publish the flight schedule. You just show up at the airport as per the timing on your ticket, in most cases, you would not even have a ticket with you, as it is with your guide. There are no signs anywhere to notify if your flight was getting delayed and no announcement system either. The staff would tell you nothing, even the guides do not know anything, it is a guessing game and a game of speculation. If you notice any ground staff around you, you had to assume that a flight was about to land. Their turnaround time was very good though, because they had such a small window of good weather, that they had to make the most of it. So, from disembarking to take off, everything was done in fifteen minutes, kudos to that. We had a similar issue at Kathmandu Domestic Airport as well, no digital boards, no announcements, some airlines had a handwritten sign on their window with a one liner. When you saw people start to leave with dropped shoulders and a sad face, you knew that their flight had been cancelled for that day. So, if anyone wanted to work on their patience levels, they just had to take a trip to Kathmandu/Ramechhap/Lukla and experience flight cancellations and reschedules, two days or may be three days in a row. It is a very different and unique experience.

30th of Sept:

When I woke up the next morning, the weather was simply beautiful. We quickly went to the airport, and to our delight we realized that our flight was second in line. The first flight had already taken off, then another flight from another airline had taken off and then there was no movement. We were at the airport at 6.30 am and by then it was 11 am and we are still waiting for our flight to land. We came to know later, that too not from the airport staff, but from fellow travellers, whose friends made it to Kathmandu that, in the morning, due to heavy air traffic at Kathmandu, there was a delay flying in and out and that was why our flight had gotten delayed. Finally, our flight landed by 11.30 am and we reached Kathmandu by 12.15 pm, only to know that Lukla airport was shut again due to bad weather. We were lucky, we got that small window to fly out from Lukla.

And by 1 pm I was at the Hotel reunited with my friends, who were waiting for me since the day before.

Back together–An old Pic from Lukla

"All's well if all ends well."
– William Shakespeare.

HANDY TIPS

Here are a few things I learned through the course of my journey that I thought I would share with you so they may serve you if you ever decided to do the EBC.

Covers 95% of essential items for the trek.

Do's–

- If you are trekking to any destination, please try and use local guides and porters. This would not only help you trek safely but also help the local community and economy.

- Please dispose your trash responsibly.

- Please carry minimum clothing on the trek. Maximum allowance to Lukla is fifteen kgs, but trust me, you can manage with ten kgs.

- Please tip generously wherever you can, especially to your guide, porter, and hotel staff on the trek and in Kathmandu.

- Please carry local currency on the trek. If the food and accommodation is part of your package, you would still need around 750-800 NPR per day, per person, on an average.

- Start early, go slow, enjoy the trek and the surroundings. It's very unlikely you will do the same trek again. A tour guide might rush you.

- It is best to exchange the currency locally in Kathmandu, you get better rate than your home country. Cash is preferred everywhere. They do accept Indian Currency as well.

- Allow couple of extra days towards the end of your trek, to factor in flight cancellations due to bad weather.

- Carry some Snickers/Mars on the trek. For your sugar intake and also to distribute it to the porters who carry eighty to ninety kgs on their back and walk for two to three days at a stretch.

- On the trek, keep yourself hydrated, drink lots of water, have food at regular intervals.

- Use water purification tablets. Please don't ignore the early signs of dehydration and high-altitude sickness.

- High altitude medical cover is a must. (3000m and above with helicopter rescue)

- Prefer vegetarian meals on the trek as meat is carried by mule or on foot and could take days to reach its destination.

- Please carry good quality rain jackets or poncho, waterproof shoes and gloves.

Don'ts–

- Do not skip acclimatisation, despite your flight cancellation.

- On the trek, do not expect luxury. Most of the facilities are very basic. Basic rooms, no power points, or common toilets, Sometimes the toilets are outside.

- Do not expect a hot shower or heaters in the room.

- Do not expect hand wash or toilet paper or water jets. It is best you carry few toilet paper rolls and hand wash with you from Namche. It gets expensive the higher you go.

- Do not carry too many clothes. A porter is allowed to carry ten to twelve kg per person but be considerate. And you don't need more than eight to ten kgs in total.

- Don't expect a smooth trek. Bad weather can put a spanner in your plans any moment. Especially the flights from and to Lukla.

SAYONARA

After the long, tiring but fulfilling trek and yet another flight cancellation, I was back in Kathmandu, two days before my return flight to Melbourne. I still had to buy some souvenirs, so I spent most of my time shopping. The same night, Nir from Ghumnajaau, our travel company, took us out for dinner at Avocado Cafe. It was a nice place with good ambience, friendly staff, and tasty food. The place had a capacity of three hundred patrons, and they looked after each and every customer very well. Throughout our stay in Nepal, only once had I had a bad meal, a pizza. But other than that, the food had been amazing, and the service was even better.

We visited so many shops, not necessarily with the intention of buying anything but simply to browse, yet the staff or owners of each shop were very informative, friendly, and never pestered us to buy from their shop. The entire approach was tourist centric, knowing that it was an integral part of their economy. And Thamel, was just the right kind of place for tourists, no matter which country they were from, it had everything for everyone. And that was what I liked about Kathmandu, Nepal. Everyone there was just so happy. I was sure, they all had their struggles, pain and sorrows but they still managed to stay happy which was very contagious.

Finally, and sadly, the unavoidable day of our return had arrived. We left the hotel and reached the airport at around 7.30 am, it was quite an opposite experience this time. Though the airport was full, people were standing in a queue, patiently waiting their turn. Everything was very smooth, and we boarded the flight to Delhi, by Air India again. Our flight from Delhi to Melbourne got delayed by two hours, so we had six hours to kill in Delhi, out of which three were consumed in clearing the security.

When we boarded the flight at 5.30 pm, we were hoping to take off by 5.45 pm but that did not happen and we were there till 6.30 pm. While we waited inside the plane, the air conditioner was not switched on. After complaining we were told that it would work only after take-off. It did eventually work after take-off just as they had confirmed. Shortly after that, there was a medical emergency on the plane. Thankfully there was a doctor onboard who helped the traveller and managed to make her feel better, but I suspect this had happened due to the air conditioner being turned off for such a long time. Again, Air India, like I said before, was very consistent in their poor facilities and poor customer service. By now, I knew, the entertainment screen did not work, so we started talking to fellow travellers to entertain ourselves, which rarely happens on other airlines.

Now back to Melbourne, the sky did not look the same, as it did back in Nepal. The surrounding mountains looked smaller than the giants, we were walking with. The small dusty trails were now replaced by four to six lane motorways. The scenic view was now replaced by suburban houses or tall towers in the CBD (Central Business District). The snow was nowhere to be seen. The mules, jopke and the porters were replaced with Utes and B Double trucks. The constant sound of flowing river water wase audible only when I turned on my water tap in the shower or in the kitchen sink. My walks were now limited to the car park, instead of six to eight hours during a trekking day. Honey lemon tea was now replaced with an overpriced coffee. I did not order my dinner until 4 pm, instead I started making it. I was now surrounded by people going to office every day and not trekkers with a shared destination, goals, and experiences. The staff at the hotels and shops were not as courteous as they were in Nepal.

Back to reality now. But one thing was very certain, I could see myself visiting Nepal again, may be in the next couple of years, may be for another adventure or just to explore some other parts of Nepal and make some more memories.

A mind that is stretched by new experience,
can never go back to its old dimensions.

GRATITUDE

For me personally, the Everest Base camp trek was a truly life changing experience. I have learned so many things in this entire process. How to nurture your dreams, how to handle challenges that life throws at you, while trying to achieve those dreams or goals. How to remain focussed and determined and positive towards your goals. How not to take things for granted.

It helped me understand and feel the pain and suffering of the people I met on the trek.

The uphill struggles were not merely physical; but were metaphors for life's challenges. The view of the sunrise over the Himalayan peaks made me realize how small yet interconnected we are with the vastness of nature—it was a humbling and awe-inspiring moment.

While the achievement was mine, it would not have been possible without the grace of God and the unwavering support and encouragement of my well-wishers.

I am deeply grateful that the Everest Base Camp trek not only challenged me physically but also awakened a passion for writing that I had not discovered before. The journey inspired me to express my thoughts and emotions in ways I had never imagined possible, and for that, I am truly thankful. It also sparked a newfound love for hiking, encouraging me to seek out trails and mountains with fresh enthusiasm.

How can I forget Santosh & Nir, our tour guides and Dig Basnet, our porter. I cannot thank them enough for their guidance and hard work throughout this journey.

Their dedication and care made this trek possible and truly unforgettable. Especially Santosh & Dig, as they were with me during the last leg of my journey, walking shoulder to shoulder in the rain and motivating me when I needed it the most. It is because of Santosh that I was able to meet Pavin and Lakhpa and learned a few valuable life lessons.

Thanks to all the hotel staffs, driver, the rescue team, doctors, nurses, and everyone who has directly or indirectly helped us complete the journey.

Thanks to my mother, who pushed me to continue the trek, after my father's sudden demise. The last few years were very tough for her, she was confined to home due to my father's illness. But she wanted me to fulfill my dream and encouraged me throughout this journey from start to finish. My father would have loved hearing about all the stories from the trek, if he were alive. My sister, my friends, my cousins, relatives, they wanted me to tick off this item from my bucket list and were wishing for my success.

I will be selfish to not thank my staff and supervisors who took care of my business while I was on the trek, not reachable most of the time. I would not have thought of going on a trek, without their assurance, support, and help.

Thanks to Kappiil and Gavin for accompanying me. I would not have done this by myself and having you around made it easier than I thought. Thank you for all the laughter, support, the music, and the fun we had. Thanks for these lifelong memories.

I am thankful to so many people encouraging me to write and publish this book. It was an unknown territory for me and their guidance and motivation helped me publish my first ever book.